The **Italian** Mama's Kitchen

The Italian Mama's Kitchen

Authentic home-style recipes

Katie and Giancarlo Caldesi

An Hachette UK Company
First published in Great Britain in 2005 by Spruce
a division of Octopus Publishing Group Ltd
2–4 Heron Quays, London E14 4JP.
www.octopusbooksusa.com

Distributed in the U.S. and Canada for Octopus Books USA
c/- Hachette Book Group USA
237 Park Avenue
New York NY 10017.

ISBN 13 978-1-84601-320-1
ISBN 10 1-84601-320-8

A CIP catalogue record for this book is available from the British Library.

Printed and bound in China

10 9 8 7 6 5 4 3

Contents

Introduction

During the writing of this book we came to realize that, although Giancarlo came from a poor background as a Tuscan farmer's boy, he had actually had a very rich culinary life. The countryside in which he lived provided a wonderful supply of fresh food that was cooked in the manner of one of the best cuisines in the world. Giancarlo doesn't remember having more than six toys during his entire childhood, and he has no memory of ever having received a single Christmas present, but he does have abundant memories of wonderful feasts, family gatherings, the comforting aromas of meals being prepared in the family kitchen—and fresh pasta, which his mother made by hand daily. Because he knew no other kind of food (lucky him), Giancarlo took for granted some of the very dishes that customers at our restaurants rave about today.

Giancarlo's *Babbo* (meaning "dad" in Italian), Adelmo (or Memmo, as his family calls him), was very much the provider. Every day, he rose with the sun and headed off to work all day in the fields. Marietta, Giancarlo's mother, looked after the house, the boys, and the animals. Much of her time was spent preparing delicious meals for her family. She always used fresh ingredients, which were readily available (and for which we pay through the nose today!), and she always used extra-virgin olive oil from the first cold pressing of the olives that grew on their farm. At harvesttime, the family gathered to pick the olives from the trees, and they'd take the olives to the local *frantoio*—or oil press—in the village. For a small fee, Giancarlo's family had their olives pressed, and returned home with bottles of thick green oil that they'd use throughout the year.

About twenty chickens, more than a dozen ducks, six geese, seven or eight cows, several pigs, at least thirty guinea hens, two cats, and sometimes a few pigeons roamed the family farm. Giancarlo's family grew wheat, barley, corn, squash, potatoes, zucchini, onions, and garlic. All of the typical Tuscan herbs, three types of lettuce, and spring onions grew in Memmo's herb garden. The trees that surrounded the farm provided plums, peaches, apricots, pears, almonds, walnuts, and figs.

Every other Sunday, Giancarlo's parents rose at 4:00 a.m. to bake bread. Although the bread kept well in the *madia*—or bread bin—the family was always pleased to have fresh bread. They baked twenty to thirty loaves each time. While the oven heated up, Marietta would shape the dough and place the loaves on planks. When the oven was hot, Giancarlo's brother and father carried the bread to the oven, pushing the planks into the oven using a wooden plate on a stick. The neighbors also used the oven, bringing their own wood for its fire. The large oven took three hours to heat, so it was good that friends were able to use it as well! Once the charcoals were glowing, they were pushed to one side of the oven and the bread was laid next to it. Brooms made of olive branches (with the leaves still on) were dipped into water and brushed over the coals to create steam and to cool the oven's temperature a bit. This created the perfect environment for a Tuscan bread called pane Toscano. The loaves were about ten inches across, crusty on the outside, and deliciously soft on the inside. This bread was eaten with every meal and used in many dishes, including zuppa di pane e pomodoro, bruschetta, and panzanella.

The hot oven was used to bake more than just bread. Meat was roasted and cakes were baked at this time as well. In Italian villages, it was traditional to have a roast and a cake for the main meal of the day on these Sundays. The whole family would go to Mass and Marietta would leave the church early to go home, take the roasted meat out of the oven, and put the cakes in. By the time the rest of the family came home, the Sunday lunch was prepared.

Tuscan villagers "ate with the seasons," using only those ingredients at their peak of freshness, a practice that we try to follow today in our restaurants and at home. With the variety available from our suppliers or in the supermarkets it's hard to refuse the choices, but frequent trips back to the markets of Italy remind us how to eat with the seasons and therefore get the best out of local produce. Over the past two years we've sold our Italian patisserie at a local farmer's market, giving us an opportunity to purchase the wonderful, just-picked produce that other vendors sell, including carrots and potatoes still covered in soil (just as we remember them from our youth), the first strawberries of summer, and tough but tasty winter cabbage. At least to this extent, we are able to continue the healthful, centuries-old tradition of eating "with the seasons." In other ways, however, our daily lives are vastly different from that of Giancarlo when he was a child.

People in the Italian countryside rose early, often at sunrise. It was usually the grandmother's job to light the fire and to prepare barley coffee, into which bread would be dipped. Milk (obtained from either a cow or a goat) was precious, and it was served to the children. Everyone attended to his or her chores for several hours. At around 10:00 a.m., the family gathered together to eat breakfast. This usually consisted of bread, in-season vegetables, homemade salami, cheese, and fruit. Lunch, usually served around 1:00 p.m., consisted of perhaps a soup, a stew, or some homemade pasta, such as tagliatelle or pici, served with a tomato and beef, chicken, or rabbit sauce. This would be followed by meat. The evening meal courses were similar to those of lunch, with fish, such as baccala, served every Friday. At every meal—even breakfast— fresh well water and a bit of wine were served.

Every day follows much the same routine on an Italian farm. For this reason, villagers look for any reason to celebrate special occasions. For Giancarlo's family, celebrations brought families and friends together to share in the cooking of feasts and meals. Marietta enjoyed both the help and the company, as she often spent her days working alone in the kitchen. Celebrations often called for special cakes and sweets, which were made at particular times of the year: ciambelloni for Easter; cenci for Carnevale; and frittelle di budino di riso for Father's Day. During the most important festivities, crostini neri would be prepared as part of a range of antipasti.

Neighbors helped each other out during harvesttimes, or when help was needed to complete other tasks—everyone was expected to return the same amount of help when it was needed. The grape harvest, known as Vendemmia, required a lot of help from neighbors—all of whom Giancarlo's mother had to feed. Sometimes she cooked for up to twenty people all by herself. At other times, however, she would be assisted by the wives, mothers, and grandmothers of men who were helping to harvest the grapes. Picking grapes is a lot of work, and the days start very early. On these days, the women served a huge breakfast, skipping lunch. The women took the meals to the men in the fields, serving them on tablecloths spread over the ground—breakfasts of salami, cheeses, preserved fish, and hunks of bread. The evening meals during Vendemmia featured fresh pasta and roasted meats.

As a young boy, Giancarlo was assigned to the kitchen rather than to the fields. He loved to watch the women work, their nimble fingers skinning rabbits, making soffritto, and preparing stuffed pasta. He jumped at the chance to help out when he was allowed, leading him to his passion for cooking and entertaining. This, in turn, led him to catering school, which was followed by thirty years as a waiter and restaurant manager. The Caldesis now run two restaurants in London—Caldesi and Caffè Caldesi. They opened La Cucina Caldesi in 2005, a school that teaches everything about Italian food and wine. In 2007 Katie and Giancarlo went on to open Caldesi in Campagna, a restaurant in Bray, Berkshire, that specializes in Italy's country cooking making the best use of local, seasonal produce.

Memmo and Marietta Caldesi (center right and far right) *with their neighbors Nello Ceccuzzi* (left) *and his mother Elide* (center left).

Chapter one
Antipasti
APPETIZERS

Crudités

Pinzimonio

The key to this dish is in the quality of the ingredients used—buy the freshest, best that you can (or better yet, grow your own). In Italy, guests are given their own little pot of dipping oil for crudités. The vegetables are placed on a big plate or stood upright in a pottery bowl in the center of the table. Katie was not impressed when she first saw this served, but after she tasted the first carrot, fresh from the Tuscan soil, she realized that the quality of the vegetables make this appetizer truly delicious. "It was the most carroty carrot I had ever tasted," she said, "as if it had been injected with carrot essence!" From that moment on, it was easy for her to understand why the first spring vegetables are eaten this way.

PREPARATION TIME: 15 minutes / **COOKING TIME:** 0 minutes / **SERVES:** 4

Extra-virgin olive oil to taste ◆ Salt to taste ◆ Freshly ground black pepper to taste Fennel bulb ◆ Large cucumber, peeled and trimmed ◆ Radishes, trimmed and cleaned Carrots, cleaned and peeled ◆ Celery stalks ◆ Small spring onions, peeled

◆

1 In a small bowl, mix together the olive oil, salt, and pepper. Set aside.

2 Using a sharp knife, cut the fennel bulb into quarters. Cut the cucumber, radishes, and carrots lengthwise into quarters. (Leave the celery and onions whole.) Place the vegetables on a serving platter.

3 Serve with the olive oil mixture and explain to guests that the mixture is to be used for dipping the vegetables. The oil can be poured into small individual bowls so that nobody worries about double-dipping!

Cucumber and Celery

Cetriolo e Sedano

This very simple pairing of vegetables is a crisp and refreshing summer treat.

PREPARATION TIME: 10 minutes / **COOKING TIME:** 0 minutes / **SERVES:** 4

1 cucumber, peeled and diced ◆ 5 celery stalks, trimmed and cut into ½-inch pieces
2 to 4 tablespoons extra-virgin olive oil ◆ Salt to taste ◆ Freshly ground black pepper to taste

◆

1 In a medium bowl, toss together the cucumber, celery, and olive oil.

2 Add salt and pepper to taste and serve immediately.

White Toast

Crostini in Bianco

This was served as an appetizer on Sundays and special occasions.

PREPARATION TIME: 10 minutes / **COOKING TIME:** 0 minutes / **SERVES:** 6

12 x ⅓-inch-thick slices baguette bread ◆ 3 tablespoons finely chopped pickled vegetables,
such as cauliflower and carrots ◆ 1 anchovy, chopped finely
½ tablespoon capers, drained and chopped finely ◆ 2 tablespoons mayonnaise (see page 15)
Freshly ground black pepper to taste

◆

1 Toast the baguette slices. In a small bowl, mix together the vegetables, anchovy, capers, and mayonnaise. Add pepper to taste.

2 Pile the mixture onto the toast and serve.

Mayonnaise

Maionaise

Nothing is better than the taste of fresh, homemade mayonnaise. It's so versatile and the entire process takes little more than 5 minutes if using a blender or food processor. Extra-virgin olive oil will produce a stronger-tasting and more flavorsome mayonnaise; however, it's best to use a lighter-tasting oil if making mayonnaise for everyday use with foods such as tuna.

PREPARATION TIME: 15 minutes / **COOKING TIME:** 0 minutes / **MAKES:** serves 8

Yolk of 2 large egg ◆ **1 teaspoon fresh lemon juice**
⅔ cup sunflower or vegetable oil ◆ **Salt to taste**

◆

1 Place the egg yolks and lemon juice in a small bowl and whisk gently until creamy and light. Whisking constantly, slowly add the oil in a steady stream until the mixture is thick and stiff, then whisk in the salt.

2 To store, transfer to a container, seal tightly, and refrigerate. This may be stored in the refrigerator for up to 3 days.

Mama says:
Add a little mustard to the mayonnaise for a delicious dip to serve with raw or hot vegetables.

Stuffed Zucchini

Zucchini Ripieni

Zucchini were plentiful as they grew in our garden, so my mother would often make stuffed zucchini on the outside oven (our only oven) every Sunday. Otherwise, everything was cooked alla brace *on the grill.*

PREPARATION TIME: 15 minutes / **COOKING TIME:** 25 minutes / **SERVES:** 6

**Extra-virgin olive oil to taste ◆ 6 large (about 8 inches long) zucchini
½ cup grated, stale bread crumbs
½ medium red or white onion, peeled and chopped finely
½ cup Italian (flat-leaf) parsley, trimmed and chopped finely
1 large garlic clove, peeled and chopped finely ◆ 1 large egg, lightly beaten
Salt to taste ◆ Freshly ground black pepper to taste**

◆

1 Preheat the oven to 350°F. Lightly grease a baking sheet with olive oil.

2 Cut the zucchini in half lengthwise. Using a spoon, hollow out each half. Chop the seeds and pulp finely.

3 In a medium bowl, mix together the bread crumbs, onion, parsley, garlic, egg, and zucchini seeds and pulp. Add salt and pepper to taste.

4 Spoon the mixture into the zucchini halves. Place the zucchini on the baking sheet. Drizzle with olive oil.

5 Bake 25 minutes. Serve warm.

Mama's Pancakes

Frittelle della Mamma

*After Mama prepared Fried Zucchini Flowers (see page 20), she used the
leftover eggs and flour from that recipe to prepare these delicious little appetizers.
They are especially good when served with a cold glass of Prosecco.*

PREPARATION TIME: 5 minutes / **COOKING TIME:** 2 minutes / **SERVES:** 4

Olive oil, for frying ◆ 1 large egg ◆ 1⅓ cups all-purpose flour ◆ 2–3 tablespoons water
½ tablespoon fresh sage finely chopped ◆ 1 tablespoon finely chopped fresh Italian
(flat-leaf) parsley ◆ 1 teaspoon salt ◆ Freshly ground black pepper to taste

1 Heat the oil in a large skillet over low heat.

2 While the oil is heating, place the egg in a
large bowl and lightly beat using a fork. Add
the flour gradually, beating constantly until
smooth. Stir in water to thin the mixture.
Stir in the sage, parsley, salt, and pepper.

3 Using a tablespoon, drop spoonfuls of the
batter into the hot oil (do not overfill the skillet).
Cook until golden brown on one side (about

1 to 2 minutes). Gently turn and cook until
golden brown on the other side (about 1 minute).
Transfer to paper towels to blot any excess oil.
Repeat the process until all the batter has
been fried.

4 Sprinkle with salt and serve immediately.

Bread with Olive Oil and Salt
Ciaccia Salata

This recipe calls for OO flour, a fine-ground Italian wheat flour that has a low extraction rate and a low ash content. It is available in some specialty food stores. If you cannot find OO flour, you can substitute it with all-purpose flour.

PREPARATION TIME: 45 minutes / **COOKING TIME:** 20 to 25 minutes / **SERVES:** 4

2¼ cups warm water ◆ 1 ounce fresh or ¾ ounce active dry yeast ◆ 6½ cups OO flour or all-purpose flour ◆ Pinch of salt ◆ Extra-virgin olive oil to taste ◆ Sea salt to taste

◆

1 Place the warm water in a bowl. Sprinkle the yeast over the water and stir until blended.

2 Place the flour in a large bowl with a pinch of salt and mix thoroughly. Make a well in the center of the flour. Slowly pour the yeast-water mixture into the well. Using a flat-bladed knife, mix thoroughly, adding more water if necessary, until the dough is soft but firm. Remove the dough from the bowl and knead for 5 to 10 minutes.

3 Grease the bowl and return the dough to the bowl. Cover with a damp towel and let sit in a warm, draft-free place for 30 minutes to 1 hour or until the dough has doubled in size.

4 Preheat the oven to 400°F.

5 Lightly grease a baking sheet with olive oil. Set aside.

6 Transfer the dough to a lightly-floured work surface. Roll the dough using a rolling pin, flattening it slightly into a ½-inch-thick oval shape or 2 small 1cm-thick oval shapes. Place the dough on the baking sheet. Drizzle with olive oil and sprinkle with sea salt.

7 Bake 20 to 25 minutes or until the crust is golden brown.

Mama says:
For added flavor, push whole, pitted olives into the top of the dough just before placing it in the oven to bake.

Fried Zucchini Flowers

Fiori di Zucca Fritti

Fresh zucchini flowers have a subtle and delicious flavor that is enhanced when they're fried. However, if you are only able to buy frozen zucchini flowers, try stuffing them with a little ricotta stuffing, made from lightly whipped egg white, ricotta, herbs, salt, and pepper. This will add flavor and interest to the dish.

PREPARATION TIME: 10 minutes / COOKING TIME: 5 minutes / SERVES: 6

**6 zucchini flowers ◆ Small bowl of all-purpose flour
2 large eggs, lightly beaten
2 cups olive oil
Salt to taste**

◆

1 Gently remove and discard the stems and stamens from each flower. Rinse the flowers carefully and pat dry with paper towels. Trim the stalks to 2 inches in length.

2 Place the flour in a shallow bowl. Dip each flower into the flour, then into the egg.

3 Place the olive oil in a deep-sided skillet to form a 1¼-inch layer of oil. Heat over medium heat.

4 Place three flowers in the skillet and fry until golden brown, turning once (about 30 seconds per side). Transfer to the paper towels to blot any excess oil. Repeat.

5 Sprinkle the flowers with salt and serve immediately.

Tuscan Garlic Bread

Fettunta

This is a great way to use bread that has gone slightly stale—something that happened quickly in the heat of summer when I was a child. It is also a good way to use bread left over from a dinner or party. Make this recipe to enjoy after everyone has gone home. This bread is best when made with a high-quality olive oil. Mind the drips! We have a family saying that you are not a Caldesi unless you have a little drip of olive oil on your chin, showing that you have enjoyed your food.

PREPARATION TIME: 5 minutes / **COOKING TIME:** 5 minutes / **SERVES:** 4

8 x 1¼-inch-thick slices Tuscan or other farmhouse-style white bread
1 large garlic clove, peeled ◆ Extra-virgin olive oil, to drizzle ◆ Salt to taste

◆

1 Toast the bread slices on both sides.

2 While still warm, lightly rub a garlic clove over the surface of one side of the toast. (For a light garlic flavor, rub only a few times.

For a more intense garlic flavor, rub several times.) Place the toast on a serving platter.

3 Drizzle olive oil over the toast. Sprinkle with salt to taste and serve.

Bruschetta with Fresh Tomato
Bruschetta di Pomodoro

This recipe is a delicious way to use ripe tomatoes when the garden produces an abundance. We prefer beefsteak tomatoes, but any variety can be used as long as the tomatoes are sweet and full of flavor. The bread may be toasted and set aside up to a few hours ahead of time, if desired. Once it is topped with oil and tomato, it should be served right away, before it becomes soggy. A delicious alternative to fresh tomato is to top the toasted bread with oven-dried tomatoes (see page 23).

PREPARATION TIME: 10 minutes / **COOKING TIME:** 3 minutes / **SERVES:** 10

10 x ½-inch-thick slices Tuscan or other farmhouse-style white bread
2 to 4 large garlic cloves, peeled ◆ Extra-virgin olive oil, to drizzle
4 large beefsteak tomatoes, cored, trimmed, and sliced thinly
Handful (about ½ cup) fresh basil, torn into pieces ◆ Salt to taste
Freshly ground black pepper to taste

◆

1 Toast the bread slices if desired. Set aside.

2 Rub a garlic clove over one side of each slice of toast. Place the slices in a single layer on a serving platter and drizzle with olive oil.

3 Place a tomato slice on top of each toast. Sprinkle the basil over the toast. Sprinkle with salt and pepper and serve immediately.

Oven-dried Tomato
Pomodori Secchi al Forno

In Tuscany I leave cherry tomatoes outside to dry in the hot sun, which takes about one day. I cover them with a fly net that lets the light through but not the insects. Oven-dried tomatoes are great served with drinks, which we often do, or squashed into foccaccia before it's baked. They are also good thrown into a salad. The best time to make these is toward the end of summer when the tomatoes are ripe, sweet, and full of flavor. Use the best quality you can find.

PREPARATION TIME: 5 minutes / **COOKING TIME:** 1½ hours / **SERVES:** 4 to 6

40 cherry tomatoes, cut in half ◆ **½ teaspoon sea salt**
1 teaspoon thyme, finely chopped

◆

1 Pre-heat the oven to 225°F.

2 Lay the tomatoes, flesh side up, on a baking tray. Sprinkle over the salt and thyme, and bake for 1½ hours.

3 Remove from the oven and allow to cool on the tray. These can be kept refrigerated for upto 2 days.

Tomato, Basil, and Mozzarella

Pomodori, Basilico e Mozzarella

You may use a variety of tomatoes—from beefsteak to Roma to cherry—for this dish. Select tomatoes that are sweet and full of flavor. The creamy texture of buffalo mozzarella perfectly complements the acidity of the tomatoes, but you may substitute another good-quality mozzarella if you prefer. If you cannot find good mozzarella, omit the cheese and use thinly sliced red onions instead.

PREPARATION TIME: 10 minutes / **COOKING TIME:** 0 minutes / **SERVES:** 6

4 large tomatoes or 16 cherry tomatoes
4 x 3-inch-wide slices buffalo mozzarella or other good-quality mozzarella
12 fresh basil leaves ◆ 3 tablespoons extra-virgin olive oil
Salt to taste ◆ Freshly ground black pepper to taste

1 Slice the tomatoes and mozzarella thinly.

2 Place the tomato and mozzarella slices on a serving platter, alternating the tomato and mozzarella slices.

3 Tear the basil leaves from the stems and tuck them between the tomatoes and mozzarella.

4 Drizzle with olive oil. Sprinkle with salt and pepper to taste. Serve at room temperature.

Zucchini, Mozzarella, and Basil Balls

Involtini de Zucchini, Mozzarella e Basilico

These pretty little rolls are perfect antipasti. Strips of grilled eggplant or roasted peppers also work well in this dish, or try a selection of all three. We make them frequently in our cookery school La Cucina Caldesi where my mother's original recipe has been perfected by Marta, who works with us. She grills the zucchini first, so that the rolls roll up more easily.

PREPARATION TIME: 15 minutes / **COOKING TIME:** 3 to 5 minutes / **SERVES:** 6 (allow 2 per person)

**2 zucchini, thinly sliced ◆ Extra-virgin olive oil, enough to drizzle
Salt and freshly ground black pepper to taste ◆ 12 bocconcini or small pieces
of mozzarella ◆ 12 leaves of fresh basil ◆ 12 cocktail sticks**

◆

1 Pre-heat the broiler. Slice the zucchini very thinly lengthwise using a potato peeler or sharp knife. Lay them onto a baking tray, drizzle with olive oil, and sprinkle with salt and pepper.

2 Place under the grill and leave for a couple of minutes, or until they start to soften and become golden. Remove and allow them to cool.

3 Put a ball of the bocconcini and a basil leaf at one end of the courgette and roll it up, then push a cocktail stick through the middle to secure.

4 Roll up the remaining bocconcini, then arrange them on a plate and serve.

Baked Onions Under the Ashes
Cipolle alla Brace

When I was a child, we made this dish in the evenings when the wood from our fire had turned to glowing embers. This dish may also be made using still-hot coal ashes.

PREPARATION TIME: 5 minutes / **COOKING TIME:** 40 to 50 minutes / **SERVES:** 4

4 medium red onions, unpeeled ◆ Extra-virgin olive oil, to drizzle
Salt to taste ◆ Freshly ground black pepper to taste
Balsamic vinegar to taste, if desired

◆

1 Bury the onions in glowing, ashy wood or charcoal embers. Cover with more embers. Cook 40 to 50 minutes or until the onion centers feel soft when squeezed gently with an oven mitt.

2 Transfer the onions to a platter. Cut into quarters and drizzle with olive oil. Sprinkle with salt and pepper to taste. If desired, drizzle with balsamic vinegar. Serve warm with crusty bread.

Prosciutto and Figs
Prosciutto e Fichi

The sweetness of fresh figs works well with the saltiness of the prosciutto in this pairing. Any figs—as long as they are of a good quality and not too woody—will combine well with any salty ham available. Memmo was very proud of his fig tree and always gave us a basket of figs to take home.

PREPARATION TIME: 5 minutes / **COOKING TIME:** 0 minutes / **SERVES:** 4

8 slices high-quality prosciutto ◆ 4 fresh figs
Fresh Tuscan bread to serve

◆

1 Arrange the prosciutto slices on a large serving dish.

2 Remove and discard the skins from the figs. Slice the top of each fig crosswise, to create four quarters that are still joined at the bottom. Stand the figs up, push open the quarters slightly, and rest the figs on the prosciutto slices.

3 Serve at room temperature with Tuscan bread.

Mama says:
Try wrapping slices of prosciutto around pieces of honeydew melon. Serve on a platter at room temperature.

Black Kale and Beans on Garlic Toast

Crostini con Cavolo Nero e Fagioli Bianchi

As a child, I loved eating this dish in the winter, when kale was at its peak.
Black kale is available at specialty food stores and at some grocery stores.

PREPARATION TIME: 6 or more hours (to allow beans to soak) plus 20 minutes
COOKING TIME: 1 hour / **SERVES:** 6

½ cup dried cannellini or other white beans ◆ Salt ◆ 1 medium tomato
1 celery stalk, trimmed ◆ 1 carrot, peeled ◆ ½ medium yellow onion, unpeeled
6 large garlic cloves, unpeeled ◆ 1 small bunch (about 5 tablespoons) fresh sage
Extra-virgin olive oil ◆ 1 black kale, trimmed and washed
12 x ⅓-inch-thick slices baguette bread ◆ Freshly ground black pepper to taste

◆

1 Place the beans in a large pot. Fill with cold water about 3 inches above the beans. Add a pinch of salt. Soak for 6 hours or overnight.

2 Drain the beans. Rinse in cold water. Place the beans in a skillet and cover with cold water.

3 Cut two slits crosswise into the top of the tomato. Add the tomato, celery, carrot, onion, 3 unpeeled garlic cloves, sage, salt, and a tablespoon of olive oil to the beans. Bring to a boil over medium-high heat. Reduce the heat to medium-low and simmer 40 minutes or until the beans are soft. Drain the beans and discard all other ingredients.

4 Place the kale in a medium skillet. Cover with water and bring to a boil over medium-high heat.

Boil 8 to 10 minutes or until the kale is just soft. Drain and set aside.

5 While the kale is boiling, toast the baguette slices. Peel the remaining 3 garlic cloves. Rub one clove onto one side of each slice of toast. Place the toast slices on a serving platter and set aside.

6 Heat 2 tablespoons oil in a skillet and add the kale, 3 peeled garlic cloves, salt, and pepper. Stir to mix and cook over low heat until the kale is heated through.

7 Use the remaining oil to drizzle onto the toast. Place a spoonful of the kale mixture on each slice. Top with a few white beans, a little oil, and pepper to taste. Serve warm or at room temperature.

Pan-Fried Porcini Mushrooms

Funghi Porcini allo Spiedo o in Padella

In the fall, I would hunt for porcini under chestnut trees in the woods with friends and family. One time, when I was out searching with some older male members of my family, I found a large number of porcini under a tree. I was so excited that I shouted out "porcini!" All of the men ran over and stole my collection of mushrooms. The moral of the story: when you find porcini, keep it to yourself!

PREPARATION TIME: 2 minutes / **COOKING TIME:** 5 minutes / **SERVES:** 2

4 tablespoons olive oil
Small handful Italian (flat-leaf) parsley, stemmed and chopped finely ◆ Salt to taste
1 medium garlic clove, peeled and chopped finely ◆ Freshly ground black pepper to taste
2 fresh, medium-sized porcini mushrooms

◆

1 In a medium bowl, mix together 2 tablespoons olive oil, the parsley, salt, garlic, and pepper.

2 Remove the mushroom stalks. Stalks can be chopped and added to a ragù or stewed meat for a mushroom flavor. Gently rub the mushrooms with the oil mixture or marinate for a stronger flavor.

3 Place 2 tablespoons olive oil in a medium skillet and heat over low heat. Gently place the mushrooms in the skillet. Pour any remaining marinade over the mushrooms. Increase the heat to medium and cook the mushrooms 2 minutes. Using a spatula, gently turn the mushrooms over. Cook until heated through.

4 Serve with the juices from the pan and pieces of fresh bread.

mama says:
if desired, the mushrooms may
be grilled instead of pan-fried.

Pecorino and Radicchio Toast

Crostini di Pecorino e Radicchio Rosso

Radicchio is a very popular vegetable in Italy, partly because it's so easy to grow. It's leafy, with a slightly bitter taste that perfectly complements the fine flavor of the pecorino and the crisp crunch of the toasted baguette.

PREPARATION TIME: 15 minutes / **COOKING TIME:** 10 minutes / **SERVES:** 6–8

**12-inch-long baguette, sliced into ½-inch slices ◆ 5 ounces radicchio, finely chopped
3 ounces (about ½ cup) grated pecorino cheese (available at specialty food stores)
Freshly ground black pepper to taste ◆ Extra-virgin olive oil to drizzle
Few sprigs of parsley, torn into pieces**

◆

1 Preheat the broiler.

2 Place baguette slices in broiler and toast until top side is golden brown (about 2 minutes). Turn and toast for another few minutes until the other side is golden brown.

3 In a medium bowl, mix together radicchio and pecorino. Add pepper to taste. Spoon mixture onto toasted baguette slices and put on a baking tray.

4 Place the baguette slices in broiler and toast 2 to 3 minutes. Transfer to a serving platter and serve immediately, drizzled with a little oil. Sprinkle with torn parsley leaves.

Tuna, Beans, and Red Onion Salad
Tonno e Fagioli

My mother served this as both an antipasti and as a lunch. It is a quick standby salad if you have canned beans. Mother never added celery or parsley, but we like the addition for a little extra bite.

PREPARATION TIME: 10 minutes / **COOKING TIME:** 0 minutes / **SERVES:** 4

6-ounce can solid-white albacore tuna (in oil or water), drained
1 red onion or 2 spring onions, finely chopped ◆ 2 to 3 tablespoons olive oil
14 ounces (about 2 cups) cannellini beans, cooked ◆ 1 small handful parsley, roughly torn
1 stick celery, finely chopped (optional) ◆ Salt and freshly ground pepper to taste

1 In a medium-sized bowl, mix together the tuna, onion, olive oil, beans, parsley, and celery, if using. Toss together until well combined.

2 Season with salt and pepper, as necessary, and serve with some salad leaves and crusty bread.

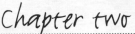

Chapter two

Contorni
SIDE DISHES

Sautéed Spinach

Spinaci Saltati

This is a very popular side order at Caldesi, our Tuscan restaurant. Our customers always want to know what makes it so tasty. We actually cook the spinach with whole garlic cloves and then remove them before serving—so customers never see the "secret" ingredient.

PREPARATION TIME: 5 minutes / **COOKING TIME:** 5 minutes / **SERVES:** 4

**2¼ pounds fresh spinach, cleaned ◆ 1 teaspoon salt
3 to 4 tablespoons extra-virgin olive oil, divided ◆ 2 large garlic cloves, peeled
Pinch of freshly grated nutmeg ◆ Freshly ground black pepper to taste**

◆

1 Remove and discard any tough stems from the spinach.

2 Fill a large saucepan with water. Add salt and bring to a boil over medium-high heat. Add the spinach to the boiling water and simmer for 3 minutes. Drain.

3 Heat 2 tablespoons olive oil in a large skillet over low heat. Add the garlic cloves, stirring to infuse the oil with garlic flavor. Add the spinach and toss to mix. Heat over medium heat until the spinach is warmed (about 2 minutes).

4 Stir in the nutmeg. Season with salt and pepper to taste. Remove the garlic cloves and transfer to a serving dish. Drizzle with the remaining 1 to 2 tablespoons olive oil and serve warm.

Sweet and Sour Green Beans
Fagiolini all'Agro

Fagiolini are the long, thin green beans we sometimes call French beans. We grew them in our garden and enjoyed them from May to August.

PREPARATION TIME: 5 minutes / **COOKING TIME:** 8 minutes / **SERVES:** 4

1 teaspoon salt ◆ 10½ ounces fresh green beans, trimmed
½ tablespoon fresh lemon juice ◆ 2 tablespoons extra-virgin olive oil
1 tablespoon white wine vinegar ◆ Freshly ground black pepper to taste
Lemon wedges, to garnish

◆

1 Fill a saucepan with water. Add salt and bring to a boil over medium-high heat.

2 Place the beans in the boiling water. Boil until the beans are tender, but not too soft (about 5 to 8 minutes). Remove from the heat and drain.

3 In a small bowl, mix together the lemon juice, olive oil, and vinegar. Add salt and pepper to taste. Pour the mixture over the green beans and toss to coat the beans. Serve with lemon wedges on a serving dish. Serve the beans warm or at room temperature.

Roasted Vegetables
Vegetali Arrostiti

For this dish, we use whatever vegetables are in season at the time. Choose a combination of carrots, zucchini, potatoes, sweet potatoes, red onions, garlic, rutabaga, or celery. Our most popular combination—potato, sweet potato, onion, and zucchini—offers a variety of flavors, colors, and textures.

PREPARATION TIME: 15 minutes / **COOKING TIME:** 25 to 30 minutes / **SERVES:** 4

Various vegetables, cleaned, trimmed, and cut into 1-inch square chunks, to fill a roasting pan in a single layer ◆ 2 sprigs fresh rosemary
4–5 fresh sage leaves ◆ 5 large garlic cloves, peeled ◆ Salt to taste
Freshly ground black pepper to taste
¼ cup plus 1 tablespoon extra-virgin olive oil

◆

1 Preheat the oven to 375°F.

2 Place the vegetables in a ceramic roasting dish or in a metal or glass roasting pan.

3 Finely chop the rosemary, sage, and garlic and mix together. Add salt and pepper to taste and spread the mixture over the vegetables. Drizzle with olive oil and toss well.

4 Bake uncovered for 25 to 30 minutes or until the vegetables are browned and tender. If they start to brown too much on top, turn and baste halfway through the cooking time.

Mama says:
For garlic roast potatoes,
follow the technique above
using potatoes instead
of vegetables.

Fava Beans with Tomato and Sage
Fave in Umido

My mother always kept tomato conserva—tomatoes preserved in jars for use during the winter—on hand for use in dishes such as this. Most of us do not preserve tomatoes anymore—this recipe calls for canned tomatoes.

PREPARATION TIME: 5 minutes / **COOKING TIME:** 30 minutes / **SERVES:** 4

**2 tablespoons extra-virgin olive oil ◆ 1 cup finely chopped yellow onion
2 large garlic cloves, peeled and chopped finely ◆ 1 pound fresh fava beans, not skinned
3 fresh sage leaves ◆ 1½ cups canned diced tomatoes, drained**

◆

1 Heat the olive oil in a large skillet over medium heat. Add the onion and sauté until soft (about 3 to 5 minutes).

2 Add the garlic, fava beans, and sage leaves to the skillet. Stir to mix and cook over medium heat until the garlic is soft (about 2 minutes).

3 Add the tomatoes to the skillet and stir to mix. Simmer 20 minutes, or until the beans are cooked.

4 Transfer to a serving dish and serve warm.

Cabbage with Garlic
Verza all'Aglio

Cabbages grew in abundance on our farm, so it was a readily available vegetable that my mother cooked frequently. By simply adding garlic, my mother made an otherwise everyday vegetable truly delicious.

PREPARATION TIME: 7 minutes / COOKING TIME: 5 minutes / SERVES: 4

**Salt to taste ◆ 1 large, whole savoy or white cabbage
¼ cup plus 1 tablespoon olive oil ◆ 2 large garlic cloves, peeled
Freshly ground black pepper to taste**

◆

1 Fill a large saucepan with water. Add salt and bring to a boil over medium-high heat.

2 While the water is coming to a boil, peel away and discard any old, tough, or damaged leaves from the cabbage. Cut the cabbage into 8 equal-sized pieces.

3 Place the cabbage in boiling water and boil about 5 minutes or until the cabbage is soft but still green. Drain.

4 Heat the olive oil in a large skillet over low heat. Add the garlic and pepper, then sauté for 1 minute.

5 Add the cabbage. Stir to mix. Transfer to a serving bowl, season with salt to taste, and serve warm.

Potato-Parmesan Mash

Puree di Patate con Parmigiano

We made this dish when we had ends of Parmesan left over—we never threw anything out and this was a good way to use up and enjoy the hard bits. You can grate right to the rind on Parmesan.

PREPARATION TIME: 15 minutes / **COOKING TIME:** 25 to 30 minutes / **SERVES:** 4

**1 pound potatoes (any variety), washed ◆ Pinch of salt ◆ ¾ cup grated Parmesan cheese
5 tablespoons butter ◆ Salt to taste ◆ Freshly ground white pepper to taste
2–4 tablespoons cold milk ◆ Parmesan shavings, to garnish**

◆

1 Place the potatoes in a large saucepan. Cover them with water, add a pinch of salt, and bring to a boil over medium-high heat. Boil until soft but not mushy. Drain. Rinse briefly in cold water. Holding them with a fork if necessary, peel off and discard the skins while the potatoes are still hot—the skins should rub off easily. Rinse the saucepan.

2 Return the potatoes to the saucepan and mash, or press them through a potato ricer into the saucepan or a mixing bowl. Add the Parmesan, 4 tablespoons butter, and salt and pepper to taste. Mash again to mix well.

3 Slowly add the milk to the potato mixture, stirring constantly, until the desired consistency is reached. Transfer the potato mixture to a serving bowl. Garnish with Parmesan shavings and the remaining butter. Serve warm.

Potato-Pumpkin Seed Mash

Puree di Patate con semi di Zucca

As a child, pumpkin season meant the coming of the annual fair at Montepulciano, money for the rides, and much excitement for the children of farmers. Roberto, my brother, and I used to carry large ripe pumpkins—which were sometimes half our weight—to the house from the garden. We'd cut holes in the top and stick our hands inside the pumpkins, giggling at the feel of their squishy contents as we pulled out their seeds. Mama would dry the seeds on big metal sheets in the outdoor bread oven, then she'd give them back to us. We cleaned and salted them, put them in little paper bags, and sold them to neighbors and visitors for a lire each—enough for two carnival rides at the fair. If we had any pumpkin seeds left over, we enjoyed them on potatoes—they add crunch and flavor to a good mash.

PREPARATION TIME: 30 minutes / **COOKING TIME:** 25 minutes / **SERVES:** 4

Pinch of salt ◆ 2¼ pounds white potatoes, washed and cut into quarters ½ cup (1 stick) butter ◆ ⅓ cup milk ◆ 1 tablespoon finely chopped Italian (flat-leaf) parsley ◆ Salt to taste ◆ Freshly ground white pepper to taste ¼ cup shelled, toasted ripe pumpkin seeds

◆

1 Fill a large saucepan with water. Add salt and bring to a boil over medium heat. Add the potatoes and boil for 10 to 15 minutes or until tender. Drain. Rinse briefly in cold water. Peel off and discard the skins while the potatoes are still hot. The skins should rub off easily.

2 Whip or mash the potatoes. Add the butter, milk, and parsley. Season with salt and pepper to taste. Mix the ingredients together thoroughly.

3 To toast the pumpkin seeds, preheat the oven to 350°F. Spread the seeds evenly onto a baking sheet. Sprinkle generously with salt to coat the seeds. Bake until golden brown and dry (about 10 minutes, but don't let them burn). Remove from the oven. Let cool. Split the outer shells and remove the seeds.

4 Transfer the potatoes to a serving dish and sprinkle with pumpkin seeds. Serve with any rich stew, such as Peposo (see page 126).

Cannellini Beans with Sage
Fagioli Bianchi

Babbo grew these—they were sometimes eaten young and fresh, simply boiled in salted water and drizzled with oil before serving. The rest would dry on the plant. We would collect these plants, take them home, spread them on a cloth, and bash them with a length of wood. This action would break open the pods, releasing the beans.

PREPARATION TIME: 6 or more hours (to allow beans to soak) plus 5 minutes
COOKING TIME: 40 minutes / SERVES: 6

2 cups dried cannellini or other white beans ◆ 2 teaspoons salt ◆ 1 medium plum tomato
1 celery stalk, trimmed ◆ 1 carrot, peeled ◆ ½ medium yellow onion, unpeeled
3 large garlic cloves, unpeeled ◆ 1 small bunch (about ½ ounce) fresh sage, plus extra to garnish ◆ 3 tablespoons extra-virgin olive oil ◆ ½ red onion, chopped finely, if desired

◆

1 Place the beans in a large pot. Cover with cold water to about 3 inches above the beans. Add 1 teaspoon salt. Let soak 6 hours or overnight.

2 Drain the beans. Rinse in cold water.

3 Place the beans in a heavy-bottomed saucepan and cover with cold water. Cut two slits crosswise into the top of the tomato and add to the beans.

4 Add the celery, carrot, onion, unpeeled garlic cloves, sage, salt, and 2 tablespoons olive oil. Bring to a boil over medium-high heat. Reduce the heat to medium-low and simmer 40 minutes or until the beans are soft. Drain the beans. Discard everything except the beans.

5 Transfer the beans to a serving dish. Drizzle with olive oil to taste. Garnish with sage leaves and red onion, if desired.

Polenta
Polenta

When the Tuscan wind blew across the fields, our tummies would cry out for more substantial food. It was polenta time, a dish that Babbo and I would make together. He would dig out the big black cauldron from storage, clean it, and hang it on a tripod above an open fire. A rounded roof tile was wedged against it to prevent it from swaying with the wind. We prepared polenta in the cauldron, taking turns pushing a wooden spoon through the mixture until it was smooth and thick. (It helped to have two people on hand to do this, as polenta must be constantly stirred for an hour!) We ate it with a good stew, such as Peposo (see page 126).

PREPARATION TIME: 2 minutes / **COOKING TIME:** 1 hour / **SERVES:** 10

28 cups water ◆ 1 tablespoon salt ◆ 6 cups polenta

1 Place the water and salt in a large stockpot. Bring to a boil over medium-high heat. Reduce the heat to medium-low.

2 Stirring constantly in a clockwise direction, slowly add the polenta, a little bit at a time.

3 Stirring constantly, cook for 1 hour.

4 Serve warm. If desired, the polenta may be stored in the refrigerator for up to 3 days.

Mama says:
To vary the polenta, stir in some grated Parmesan cheese, add some cooked Porcini mushrooms (fresh or dried), or drizzle over some truffle oil.

Artichoke and Pea Casserole

Carciofi e Piselli in Umido

We enjoyed this dish during the late summer season, using fresh artichokes and peas. In winter preserved artichokes in jars and canned or frozen peas can be used instead. Drain and rinse the preserved artichokes well. If you are using canned peas, they are already cooked and are often sweetened, so omit the sugar. Although we ate this dish as a prelude to meat, it makes a good vegetarian dish, especially when accompanied by eggs.

PREPARATION TIME: 30 minutes / **COOKING TIME:** 10 minutes / **SERVES:** 4

2¼ pounds peas ◆ 1 white onion, finely chopped
1 clove garlic, peeled and crushed ◆ Salt and freshly ground pepper to taste
¼ cup olive oil ◆ 9-ounce can whole tomatoes, chopped
8 small fresh artichokes, cleaned, boiled, and cut in half
1 teaspoon superfine sugar

◆

1 Cook the peas in boiling water until just done. Drain and put aside.

2 Meanwhile, heat the oil in a large skillet over a medium heat. Add the chopped onion, garlic, salt, and pepper, and when the onions are softened, add the chopped tomatoes and bring up to the boil. Simmer for a couple of minutes.

3 Add the cooked peas and artichokes and simmer for 5 minutes. The peas will darken and the flavors will amalgamate. If the mixture looks too dry, add a little water or stock. Adjust the seasoning as necessary, adding the sugar to taste, and serve.

Mama says:
Poach an egg in the liquid in the skillet with the artichoke and peas, then serve with crusty bread.

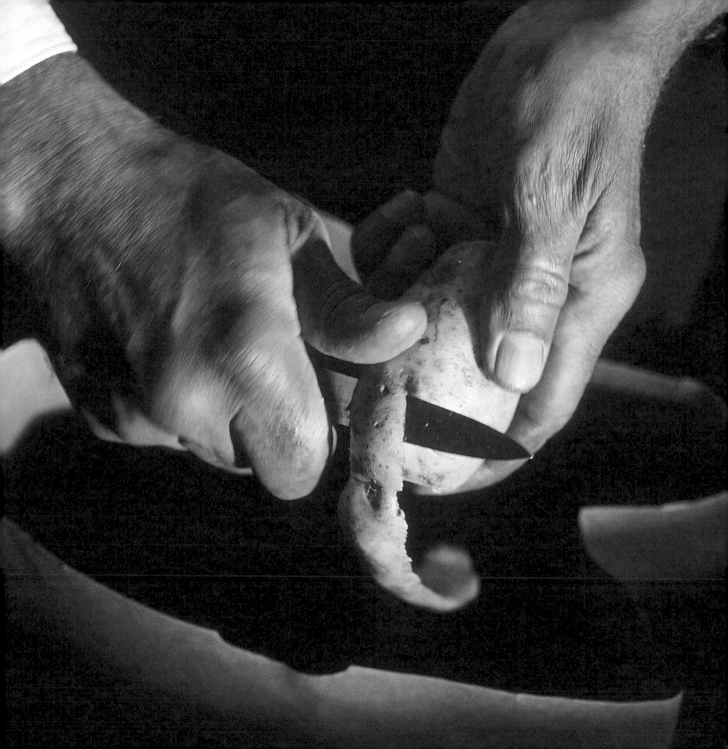

chapter three
Primi
FIRST DISHES

Chicken Stock

Brodo di Gallina

This recipe is a fine example of how my mother made use of everything that was available to us. Nothing was ever wasted in our family kitchen. We kept hens on the farm for their eggs. Hens were cooked when they stopped producing eggs. First, they would be used to make this delicious, thick stock, which was used in a variety of soups and sauces. Then, the flesh of the hen was used to make Gallina con Uva e Pinoli (Hen with Grapes and Pine Nuts). This stock gets its flavor from boiled hen—the bones give it a depth of flavor that is the hallmark of Tuscan cooking. It may be refrigerated up to 4 days or frozen up to 30 days. My mother tied the parsley and peppercorns into a small cheesecloth bag to stop the parsley breaking up and the peppercorns escaping, but you don't need to do this.

PREPARATION TIME: 10 minutes / **COOKING TIME:** 4 hours / **MAKES:** about 16 cups

**1 small bunch (about ½ ounce) Italian (flat-leaf) parsley ◆ ½ teaspoon black pepper
4-pound hen, cleaned and cut into four pieces (ask your butcher to do this)
1 medium yellow onion ◆ 3 celery stalks ◆ 1 large carrot ◆ 4 bay leaves
12 black peppercorns ◆ 4 cloves ◆ 1 teaspoon salt**

◆

1 Place the parsley and peppercorns on a piece of cheesecloth, then using kitchen string, tie the ends of the cheesecloth together to make a bag.

2 Place 16 cups water in a large stockpot. Add all the other ingredients. Bring to a boil over medium-high heat.

3 Reduce the heat to medium-low and simmer 4 hours, skimming the surface occasionally to catch and discard the residue and foam. Add

extra water to the broth, making sure that the original level of broth is maintained throughout.

4 Drain the stock through a strainer, discarding the vegetables and reserving the flesh for further use in other recipes.

Vegetable Stock
Brodo di Verdure

This stock is used in many soups and stews. It's so important to cook with a good-quality vegetable stock. This can be refrigerated up to 4 days or frozen up to 30 days.

PREPARATION TIME: 5 minutes / **COOKING TIME:** 20 minutes / **MAKES:** 9 cups

12 cups cold water ◆ 1 medium yellow onion ◆ 3 celery stalks ◆ 2 medium carrots
1 small bunch (about ½ ounce) Italian (flat-leaf) parsley leaves ◆ 2 medium tomatoes
1 medium potato, peeled ◆ 1 teaspoon salt ◆ 6 black peppercorns

◆

1 Place all the ingredients in a stockpot. Cover and bring to a boil over medium-high heat.

2 Reduce the heat and simmer 20 minutes. Drain the stock into a bowl. Discard vegetables.

Soffritto
Soffritto

This is the base for a great many Tuscan sauces, soups, and casseroles. Added to other ingredients, it gives a dish a deep, sweet, herbed flavor. Even today, the scent of cooking soffritto reminds me so much of the delicious aromas that wafted out of Tuscan homes as mealtime approached.

PREPARATION TIME: 10 minutes / **COOKING TIME:** 10 minutes / **MAKES:** 2 cups

½ cup extra-virgin olive oil ◆ 4 celery stalks, trimmed and chopped finely
2 medium carrots, trimmed, peeled, and chopped finely
1 medium yellow onion, peeled and chopped finely ◆ 4 bay leaves
2 large garlic cloves, lightly crushed, so they remain whole ◆ 1 sprig fresh rosemary
Salt to taste ◆ Freshly ground black pepper to taste

◆

1 Heat the olive oil in a skillet over medium-low heat. Add all the other ingredients and cook, stirring occasionally, until the vegetables are soft but not mushy (about 15 minutes).

2 Remove and discard the rosemary sprig, garlic, and bay leaves.

3 Store for up to 4 days in the refrigerator and add to sauces, soups, and casseroles before cooking.

Tomato and Bread Soup
Zuppa di Pane e Pomodoro

We used leftover, overripe tomatoes to make this soup—they were sweet and delicious. Our bread went stale very quickly without salt as a preservative, so this was a perfect opportunity to use it.

PREPARATION TIME: 20 minutes / COOKING TIME: 15 minutes / SERVES: 4

1 loaf Tuscan or other farmhouse-style white bread (about 1 pound)
½ cup plus 2 tablespoons extra-virgin olive oil, plus extra for drizzling
6 to 7 large garlic cloves, peeled ◆ 10 large overripe tomatoes, skinned
1 handful (about ½ cup) fresh basil, torn into small pieces
1 cup Vegetable Stock (see page 53)

1 Place the bread in a large bowl. Cover with cold water and soak quickly. Remove the bread from the bowl, thoroughly squeeze excess water from it, and set aside.

2 Heat the oil in a large skillet over medium heat and add the garlic cloves.

3 Remove and discard the tomato seeds. Chop the tomatoes finely and add to the skillet with 2 tablespoons torn basil leaves. Cook for 10–15 minutes, stirring frequently.

4 Tear the bread into bite-sized pieces, then add them to the tomatoes. Add the Vegetable Stock.

5 Using a fork, whisk the mixture to break up the tomatoes and bread. Cook, stirring occasionally, until heated through (about 10 minutes). Remove from the heat and stir in all but 1 tablespoon of the remaining basil leaves.

6 Pour the soup into individual serving bowls. Sprinkle the remaining basil leaves in equal amounts over each serving. Drizzle with olive oil and serve hot.

Cream of Vegetable Soup
Passata di Verdure

*My family made this soup often, using any vegetables that were fresh and available.
Any seasonal, leftover vegetables were combined and the quantities always varied.
This is one combination that we enjoyed frequently.*

PREPARATION TIME: 15 minutes / **COOKING TIME:** 40 minutes / **SERVES:** 4

**2 medium carrots, trimmed and peeled ◆ 2 small zucchini, trimmed
3 small potatoes ◆ 1 small bunch (about ½ ounce) Italian (flat-leaf) parsley
2 tablespoons extra-virgin olive oil ◆ 2 bay leaves ◆ 3 large garlic cloves, peeled
4 cups Chicken Stock (see page 52) ◆ ½ cup fresh peas ◆ Salt and pepper to taste**

◆

1 Cut the carrots, zucchini, and potatoes into ¾-inch cubes.

2 Place the parsley on a piece of cheesecloth. Using kitchen string, tie the ends of the cheesecloth together to form a bag.

3 Heat the olive oil in a large saucepan over low heat. Add the carrots, zucchini, and potatoes and sauté for 10 minutes. Add the bay leaves and garlic. Stir well. Cook for 3 minutes.

4 Pour the stock into the saucepan. Add the parsley and peas. Simmer over low heat for 30 minutes.

5 Remove and discard the parsley and bay leaves. Transfer the stock to a blender or a food processor. Blend until the mixture is of a consistency you desire. Return the soup to the saucepan to reheat before serving and add salt and pepper to taste. Store in the refrigerator for up to 3 days.

Pasta and Chickpea Soup

Zuppa di Ceci e Pasta

This is a hearty, full-flavored, warming soup that Mama made us for lunch during the winter. We used a short, ridged pasta called ditalini rigate, *but any type of short (¾ inch long or less) pasta is fine. This soup has become a favorite in our restaurant Caldesi in Campagna in Bray and the recipe is from Gregorio Piazza, our Head Chef.*

PREPARATION TIME: 6 or more hours (to allow chickpeas to soak)
COOKING TIME: 30 minutes / **SERVES:** 6 to 8

2 cups dried chickpeas ◆ 2 teaspoons salt, plus extra to taste
¼ cup extra virgin olive oil, plus extra to drizzle ◆ 2 medium tomatoes ◆ 1 garlic clove
2 stems fresh sage, leaves only ◆ 1 cup Soffritto (see page 54) ◆ 1 tablespoon tomato paste
Freshly ground white pepper to taste ◆ Chicken or Vegetable Stock (about ¾ cup)
½ cup uncooked short pasta

◆

1 Place the chickpeas in a large pot. Cover with cold water so that the water is about 3 inches above the chickpeas. Add 2 teaspoons salt. Soak for 6 hours or overnight.

2 Drain the chickpeas. Rinse in cold water. Place the chickpeas in a heavy-bottomed saucepan and with 4 cups cold water. Cut two slits crosswise into the tops of the tomatoes and add to the chickpeas. Add the garlic, sage, and salt to taste.

3 Bring the mixture to a boil over medium-high heat. Reduce the heat to low and simmer until the chickpeas are soft (1½ hours). While the chickpeas are cooking, make the Soffritto (see page 54).

4 Drain the chickpeas, reserving the liquid. Add the chickpeas to the Soffritto, and cook over medium heat for about 5 minutes, stirring constantly, and then add the reserved liquid, tomato paste, and season to taste. Bring the mixture to a light simmer.

5 Using a large spoon, transfer about one third of the mixture to a food processor and blend until smooth. Return this to the saucepan. Add the pasta along with the stock, as required. There should be enough liquid to cook the pasta.

6 Cook until the pasta is al dente. Serve in bowls and drizzle with olive oil.

Homemade Bread
Pane Fatto in Casa

This was part of our staple diet—we ate bread with every meal. Tuscan bread is made without salt. Adjust the water by a tablespoon either way, because not all flours have the same absorbency.

PREPARATION TIME: 30 minutes, plus 1½ to 2 hours to allow dough to rest
COOKING TIME: 1 hour / **MAKES:** 1 loaf

**2½ cups warm water ◆ 1 ounce fresh yeast or ¾-ounce packet dried yeast
6⅓ cups OO flour (available at specialty food stores) or all-purpose flour**

◆

1 Place ¼ cup water in a large bowl. Stir in the yeast. Mix well until all lumps of yeast have disappeared.

2 Put the flour in a large bowl and make a well in the center. Add the yeast mixture and the rest of the water, little by little, mixing as you go.

3 Using your fingers, form a ball with the dough. Remove the dough from the bowl and knead on a floured surface for 10 minutes.

4 Cover the dough with a kitchen towel. Place it in a warm, draft-free place and let sit until the dough has doubled in size (about 1½–2 hours, depending on the warmth and humidity of the room).

5 Preheat the oven to 350°F.

6 Using your hands, remove the air from the dough by pounding it. Shape the dough into a round loaf and place it on a baking tray or in an oiled bread pan. Make a cross in the top with a sharp knife—this helps it to rise. Leave until the dough has doubled in size again.

7 Bake 40 to 50 minutes or until the loaf is golden brown and sounds hollow when tapped on its underside.

Franca's Tuscan Bean and Vegetable Soup

Zuppa Toscana alla Franca

*My mother made this frequently, as did most Tuscan housewives of her time
(many still do today). There are hundreds of variations of this dish, and all cooks
have their favorite list of ingredients to use. Recently our friend Franca Buonamici,
a pastaiola (a person who makes and sells fresh pasta), cooked for us.
Her dish reminded me so much of my mother's that I asked her for the recipe.
She has graciously permitted me to reprint it here.*

PREPARATION TIME: 6 hours or more (to allow beans to soak) plus 20 minutes
COOKING TIME: 1 hour / **SERVES:** 10

4 cups dried cannellini beans ◆ 2 teaspoons salt ◆ 4 large garlic cloves, peeled
4 fresh sage leaves ◆ 1 medium-sized savoy or white cabbage ◆ 5 medium zucchini,
trimmed ◆ 2 medium potatoes, boiled ◆ 1 cup raw squash, peeled
1 black kale ◆ 6 ounces sweet chard, washed and roughly chopped ◆ 4 tablespoons extra-
virgin olive oil ◆ 1 leek, trimmed ◆ 2 dried, mild red chilies
1 sprig fresh thyme, finely chopped ◆ Peel of ½ organic lemon, finely chopped
1 tablespoon tomato paste ◆ Pinch of freshly grated nutmeg
Freshly ground black pepper to taste ◆ 20 x ½-inch-thick slices baguette bread

◆

1 Place the beans in a large pot. Cover with cold
water to about 3 inches above the beans. Add
1 teaspoon salt, 2 garlic cloves, and sage leaves.
Let the beans soak 6 hours or overnight.

2 Place the pot over medium heat. Cook the
beans 30 to 40 minutes or until soft.

3 Drain the beans. Reserve the cooking liquid.
Transfer three quarters of the beans to a blender
or a food processor and blend until smooth. Set
aside the remaining beans.

4 Remove the tough outer cabbage leaves and
cut the cabbage, zucchini, potatoes, and squash

into 1-inch cubes. Remove the tough outer leaves of the kale and cut the kale and chard into 1-inch-thick slices. Place the vegetables in a large, heavy-bottomed saucepan. Add the olive oil and reserved cooking liquid. Bring to a gentle simmer over low heat. Simmer 15 minutes.

5 While the mixture is simmering, finely chop the leek, chilies, thyme, and 1 garlic clove.

6 Add the leek, chilies, thyme, finely chopped garlic, lemon peel, tomato paste, nutmeg, and pepper to the soup.

7 Stir to mix. Simmer 15 minutes. Add the remaining beans.

8 While the soup is simmering, toast the bread. Rub the remaining garlic clove over both sides of each slice. Place two slices of toast in the bottom of each of ten soup bowls.

9 Adjust the soup's seasonings, if desired. Pour the soup over the toast in the bowls. Drizzle with a bit of olive oil and serve hot.

Mama says:
Cannellini beans soak up and retain a great deal of flavor due to their fluffy texture, so they are perfect for this soup recipe. Dried cannellini beans will need to be soaked for a few hours to soften them before using, but you can buy canned beans if you are short on time.

Tomato, Cucumber, and Bread Salad
Panzanella

On hot summer days, Mama would make panzanella, a cool, refreshing salad that made good use of fresh herbs from the garden and the previous day's leftover bread. This salad makes either a nice first course or a light lunch. Experiment with different types of bread to find one that most closely resembles our Tuscan bread. Be sure to serve the salad as soon as it is prepared; the bread should be soft and spongy, not soggy.

PREPARATION TIME: 30 minutes / **COOKING TIME:** 0 minutes / **SERVES:** 6 as a starter

**Half a medium-sized loaf of stale Tuscan or similar farmhouse-style white bread
1 handful basil leaves to taste ◆ 4 celery stalks, chopped coarsely
1 small cucumber, peeled and chopped coarsely ◆ 4 medium tomatoes, chopped coarsely
1 heaping tablespoon red onion, chopped coarsely, or 4 spring onions, chopped coarsely
12 radishes, trimmed and quartered ◆ 1 handful (about ½ ounce) Italian (flat-leaf) parsley,
stemmed and chopped coarsely ◆ ¼ cup plus 2 tablespoons extra-virgin olive oil
2 tablespoons white wine vinegar ◆ Salt to taste ◆ Freshly ground black pepper to taste**

1 Tear the bread into large chunks. Place in a large bowl, cover with cold water, and let soak 30 seconds.

2 Remove the bread from the bowl and squeeze out excess water. (The bread should feel spongy and should spring back into shape. It should not be soggy.) Rinse and dry the bowl. Tear the bread into bite-sized pieces and return to the bowl.

3 Set aside a few basil leaves to garnish. Tear the remaining leaves into small pieces.

4 Add the torn basil leaves, celery, cucumber, tomatoes, onion, radishes, and parsley to the bread. Toss thoroughly to mix. Set aside.

5 In a small bowl, mix together the olive oil and vinegar, stirring quickly with a fork. Pour the oil and vinegar over the tomato-bread mixture. Add salt and pepper to taste and toss to mix.

6 Transfer to individual serving dishes. Garnish each dish with a few shredded leaves of hand-torn basil and serve immediately.

Saffron Risotto

Risotto allo Zafferano

This is delicious as a first course, as is called for here, but it's also wonderful as an accompaniment to meat or as a filling for Risotto Stuffed Peppers (see page 98). Buy the best-quality saffron you can afford. The better the quality of saffron, the less you need. The more inferior the saffron, the less flavor, so you will need to add more to compensate. Adjust the amount accordingly.

PREPARATION TIME: 5 minutes / **COOKING TIME:** 20 minutes / **SERVES:** 6

¾ cup (1½ sticks) butter, softened ◆ 1 medium yellow onion, peeled and chopped finely ◆ 5¼ cups arborio rice ◆ 3¾ cups Chicken Stock (see page 52) ◆ Salt to taste
½ teaspoon high-quality saffron threads

◆

1 Melt 4 tablespoons (½ stick) butter in a medium saucepan over medium-low heat. Add the onion and sauté until golden.

2 Add the rice. Cook, stirring constantly, until the rice is lightly browned.

3 Stirring constantly, add a bit of the Chicken Stock and salt to taste. When the risotto begins to thicken, add a bit more stock. Repeat, if necessary, until the risotto has cooked for 10 minutes.

4 Stirring constantly, add the saffron. Repeat step 3, stirring constantly until all the stock is used and the risotto is thick and creamy (about 10 minutes more).

5 Remove from the heat and stir in the remaining butter. Transfer to a serving dish and serve warm.

Risotto with Tiny Mushrooms
Risotto di Chiodini

Tiny wild mushrooms are known as chiodini (little nails) in Tuscany. Elsewhere, these small mushrooms are called fiammiferi, or matchstick mushrooms (a reference to their thin bodies and small heads). They are readily available in the fields of Italy. If they are not available, use another small, thin, strongly flavored variety.

PREPARATION TIME: 5 minutes / COOKING TIME: 20 minutes / SERVES: 4

2 tablespoons extra-virgin olive oil ◆ 1 medium yellow onion, peeled and chopped finely
1½ cups tiny wild mushrooms, cleaned and chopped coarsely
2 large garlic cloves, peeled and chopped finely ◆ ½ cup dry white wine
4 cups arborio rice ◆ 4 cups Vegetable Stock (see page 53) ◆ ½ cup grated Parmesan
Butter, to garnish ◆ Parmesan shavings, to garnish

1 Heat the olive oil in a large saucepan over medium-low heat. Add the onions and mushrooms. Sauté, stirring occasionally, until the onion is soft (2 to 5 minutes). Add the garlic and sauté 30 seconds.

2 Add the wine and risotto to the onion mixture. Stir well, until the wine has been absorbed.

3 Stirring constantly, add a bit of the vegetable stock. When the risotto begins to thicken, add a bit more stock. Repeat, stirring constantly, until all the stock is used and the risotto is thick and creamy (about 20 minutes).

4 Transfer to a serving bowl, garnish with butter and Parmesan shavings, and serve warm.

Fresh Pasta Dough

Pasta Fresca

When people think of Italy, the first association that comes to mind is pasta. Dried pasta nowadays is of a very high quality; however, nothing tastes quite like homemade pasta, and it's much easier to make than you might think.

PREPARATION TIME: 1 hour / **COOKING TIME:** 0 minutes / **MAKES:** about 14 ounces to 1 pound

4½ cups OO flour (available in specialty food stores and in some grocery stores)
3 medium free-range eggs, preferably from corn-fed hens (for color), lightly beaten
About ¼ cup water

◆

1 Pour the flour into a mound on a flat surface. Make a well in the center of the mound.

2 Break the eggs into the center of the well and pour in the water. Using a flat-bladed knife, gradually mix together the eggs, flour, and water. Keep stirring together in the center of the well, incorporating the flour gradually. When the dough has become like a thick paste, use your hands to incorporate more of the flour. There will still be some surplus flour remaining around the outside.

3 When most of the dough has come together but a lot of smaller crumbs still remain, take all the crumbs and the surplus flour and sieve them. Add the sifted crumbs to the dough and knead to blend them in. Sprinkle the sifted flour onto the dough as needed to prevent it from sticking to your hands or to the surface. Use the minimum amount of flour possible; do not make the dough too dry.

4 Knead until the dough is well blended and firm but still flexible. Don't worry if you haven't used all the flour.

5 Place a bowl over the dough (to prevent it from drying out) and let sit 20 minutes. If you still have any crumbs and flour left over, sieve the flour again, this time discarding the bits and reusing the flour for rolling out. (Mama would never discard anything; she would have saved the bits and added them to a thin soup.)

Fresh Pici, Montepulciano-Style
Pici di Montepulciano

Pici, a thick spaghetti that is hand-rolled on a wooden board, is a hallmark of Tuscan cuisine. A true "peasant" dish, pici is made with some of the least expensive and most widely available ingredients. As children, we thought it was utterly delicious, and I still do. In fact, my mouth waters just thinking about it. It is traditionally made without eggs, as poorer Italian families couldn't afford eggs or didn't have eggs available to them. We had chickens, so we incorporated an egg to enrich the pasta. Because it takes a while to prepare, my mother used to enlist my help. This is a wonderful recipe to introduce children to the art of pasta-making. Our own children love to help make pici (they call it "worm pasta").

PREPARATION TIME: 1 hour / **COOKING TIME:** 10 minutes / **MAKES:** about 1½ pounds

3½ cups strong flour ◆ Pinch of salt
1 large egg ◆ ½ cup water

◆

1 In a large bowl, mix together the flour and salt. Pour the mixture in a mound onto a pastry board or other work surface. Make a well in the center of the mound.

2 Place the egg in the well. Mix the flour and egg, adding water a little at a time, until the dough is firm but flexible. Add a little more water if necessary.

3 Knead the dough until it springs back to the touch. Let it rest for 20 minutes.

4 Using a rolling pin lightly dusted in flour, roll out the dough until it measures about ⅓ inch thick. Using a sharp knife, cut the dough into ½-inch-wide strips. Roll the strips into thick, spaghetti-like strands (about ⅛ inch wide) on a lightly floured surface.

5 To cook, bring a large saucepan of salted water to a boil. Add the pici and cook until softened, 7 to 10 minutes, depending on the width of the pasta.

6 Drain and serve with the sauce of your choice.

Pici with Bread Crumbs, Garlic, and Parmesan

Pici alle Briciole

This is an extremely popular, traditional Tuscan dish. It's quick to make and is also very cheap, so it's ideal for serving to a large number of people.

PREPARATION TIME: 5 minutes / **COOKING TIME:** 7 minutes / **SERVES:** 4

1 teaspoon salt, plus extra to taste ◆ 18 ounces Fresh Pici (see page 69)
¼ cup plus 2 tablespoons extra-virgin olive oil
4 cups stale, dried Tuscan or similar farmhouse-style white bread crumbs
2 large garlic cloves, peeled and chopped finely ◆ Pinch of freshly ground black pepper
1 bunch (about ½ ounce) Italian (flat-leaf) parsley, trimmed and chopped coarsely
1 cup grated Parmesan, plus extra to garnish

◆

1 Fill a large saucepan with water. Add a pinch of salt. Bring to a boil over medium-high heat.

2 Place the pici in the boiling water. Cook until al dente (10 to 15 minutes, depending on the thickness of the pici).

3 While the pici is cooking, heat the olive oil in a large saucepan. Add the bread crumbs, garlic, remaining salt, and pepper. Sauté, stirring frequently, until the bread crumbs are golden brown (2 to 5 minutes).

4 Drain the pici. Add to the bread crumb mixture. Add the parsley and Parmesan. Toss to mix.

5 Transfer to individual pasta bowls. Serve with extra grated Parmesan and, if desired, extra olive oil.

Pici with Garlic and Tomatoes
Pici all'Aglione

Aglione *means "big garlic." As a young man, I soon realized that girlfriends were not impressed with me after I had eaten this dish—but the taste was sensational.*

PREPARATION TIME: 10 minutes / COOKING TIME: 20 minutes / SERVES: 4

¼ cup plus 2 tablespoons extra-virgin olive oil
1 medium yellow onion, peeled and chopped finely
6 large garlic cloves, peeled and chopped finely ◆ 3½ cups diced tomatoes
2 teaspoons salt ◆ Pinch of freshly ground black pepper
14 ounces Fresh Pici (see page 69) ◆ 3 tablespoons grated Parmesan

◆

1 Heat the olive oil in a large saucepan over medium-low heat. Add the onion and sauté until soft. Add the garlic and sauté 2 minutes, taking care not to let the garlic burn. Stir in the tomatoes, salt, and pepper. Cook 20 minutes, adding a little water if necessary to keep it from drying.

2 While the sauce is cooking, fill a large saucepan with water. Add the remaining salt. Bring to a boil over medium-high heat.

3 When the sauce has cooked 10 minutes, place the pici in boiling water. Cook until al dente (about 10 minutes, depending on the width of the pasta strands). Drain.

4 When the sauce has cooked 20 minutes, add the pici. Toss well to coat the pici thoroughly in the sauce. Transfer to large, individual pasta bowls. Top with a little grated Parmesan and serve immediately.

Fresh Long Pasta
Pasta Lunga

Although short pasta may be made using a pasta machine, long pasta, such as tagliatelle or pappardelle, is made the old-fashioned way—by hand.

PREPARATION TIME: 5 minutes / **COOKING TIME:** 5 minutes / **MAKES:** about 14 ounces to 1 pound

Flour, to dust work surface ◆ 1 quantity Fresh Pasta Dough (see page 66)

1 Dust a pastry board or other work surface, rolling pin, and pasta dough with flour to prevent sticking.

2 Divide the dough into quarters. Place one quarter on the work surface. To prevent drying, place the remaining quarters under a bowl or wrap in plastic wrap and set aside.

3 Using a heavy rolling pin, roll out the pasta into a rectangle; it should be thin enough to see your hand through it.

4 Fold over one edge of the dough, making a flap of about 2 inches. Continue folding the flap, sprinkling flour over the surface to prevent it from sticking to itself, until reaching the end of the pasta sheet. The pasta should resemble a flattened Swiss roll. Be generous with the flour.

5 Using the remaining dough, repeat steps 3 to 5.

6 Using a sharp knife, cut the pasta into long strips of any width desired—make tagliolini (thin 1/16-inch-wide ribbons), fettucine (1/4-inch-wide ribbons), tagliatelle (1/2-inch-wide ribbons), or pappardelle (fat 3/4-inch-wide strips).

7 The pasta is too wet to store in the refrigerator, but can be dried by laying it over a stick or flat on a board and allowing it to air-dry. Use within 3 to 4 days. It can be frozen for up to 30 days, if dried first.

8 Bring a saucepan of salted water to a boil and add the fresh pasta to cook for about 5 minutes, depending on its width. Drain and serve.

Pasta Stuffed with Ricotta and Herbs
Pasta Ripiene di Ricotta e Erbe Estive

My father kept an herb garden just outside the house. Although Mama was the cook, my father was the provider. His garden was full of sage, parsley, basil, rosemary, oregano, and wild fennel. Added to fresh ricotta, the herbs from Babbo's garden made for a wonderful pasta filling. Any combination of soft-leaf herbs may be used to prepare this filling. We are particularly fond of using basil, thyme, and Italian (flat-leaf) parsley.

PREPARATION TIME: 45 minutes / **COOKING TIME:** 5 minutes / **SERVES:** 6 as a starter, 4 as a main dish

FILLING
1 cup ricotta ◆ ¼ cup grated Parmesan
heaping ½ cup mixed fresh herbs, chopped finely ◆ Freshly grated nutmeg to taste
Salt to taste ◆ Freshly ground black pepper to taste
½ quantity of Fresh Pasta Dough (see page 66)

◆

1 Make the filling in a medium bowl, combining all the ingredients. Adjust the seasoning to taste and set aside.

2 Make the pasta. Divide the pasta into quarters. Place one quarter on a lightly floured pastry board or other work surface. Set aside the remaining quarters under a bowl to prevent drying.

3 By hand or using a pasta machine, roll out the pasta to form a long, thin, rectangular strip.

4 Starting about 1¼ inches from one end of the pasta strip, place roughly 1 teaspoon of filling in the center of the pasta. Place another teaspoon of filling about 2 inches from the first teaspoon of filling. Repeat and continue until reaching the end of the pasta strip.

5 Fold one long edge of the pasta over to meet the opposite edge. Gently press the pasta to remove excess air and to seal the filling into the pasta.

6 Using the remaining dough quarters, repeat steps 3 to 5.

7 Using a round cutter or a wineglass, cut out semicircles of pasta, working along the edge of the folded pasta sheets to produce semicircular pasta parcels containing the sealed-in filling.

8 Fill a large saucepan with water. Add a pinch of salt. Bring to a boil over high heat.

9 Gently place the filled pasta in the boiling water. Reduce heat to medium-high and cook for about 7 minutes or until the pasta is soft but not floppy or mushy.

10 While the pasta is cooking, make a sauce. Try the Butter and Mint Sauce recipe (see page 91) for a rich but refreshing flavor.

11 Drain the pasta. Place in the sauce and gently toss to coat thoroughly. Transfer to a serving dish, garnish with Parmesan, and serve immediately.

12 Filled pasta may be stored in fine semolina, refrigerated, and used within 1 hour. Be sure to store the pasta in separate layers, otherwise the parcels will stick together. If freezing, also store in fine semolina for up to 30 days.

Mama says:
Although ricotta is a popular ingredient in filled pasta dishes, don't just save it for savory meals. Combine it with blueberries, melon, and a sprinkling of sugar for a delicious breakfast treat.

Spaghetti with Anchovies and Onions
Pasta Acciughe Cipolle

This has to be one of the quickest and easiest pasta recipes ever—and is surprisingly delicious for a dish with such simple origins. The sweetness of the onions blends perfectly with the salty anchovies.

PREPARATION TIME: 5 minutes / **COOKING TIME:** 15 minutes / **SERVES:** 4

1 teaspoons salt ◆ 10 ounces uncooked spaghetti ◆ 4 tablespoons extra-virgin olive oil, plus extra to drizzle ◆ ½ red onion, finely chopped ◆ 8 anchovies, roughly chopped Freshly ground black pepper to taste ◆ Grated Parmesan

◆

1 Fill a large saucepan with water. Add the salt and bring to a boil over medium-high heat. Place the spaghetti in the water and cook until al dente.

2 While the spaghetti is cooking, heat the olive oil in a large frying pan and sauté the chopped onion. Let it soften and become transparent.

3 Add the chopped anchovies and a generous twist of black pepper, then fry with the onions for a couple of minutes. Remove from the heat.

4 Drain the spaghetti. Add it to the frying pan with the onion mix and toss well. Serve in warmed bowls with an extra drizzle of olive oil and a scattering of grated Parmesan.

Mama says:
Add some chopped
chili to the mix for
an extra kick.

Spaghetti with Garlic, Rosemary, and Porcini Mushroom

Spaghetti con Aglio, Rosmarino e Funghi Porcini

Porcini mushrooms were treasured in my family when I was growing up. The addition of this delectable ingredient brought out the flavor in any dish, no matter how few other ingredients we had to prepare our meals. If you cannot find fresh porcini use a selection of other wild mushrooms instead.

PREPARATION TIME: 5 minutes / COOKING TIME: 10 minutes / SERVES: 4

1 teaspoon salt, plus extra to taste ◆ 10 ounces uncooked spaghetti ◆ 3 tablespoons extra-virgin olive oil ◆ 1 large, fresh porcini mushroom or 14 ounces wild mushrooms, brushed clean and chopped coarsely ◆ 1 sprig rosemary ◆ Freshly ground black pepper to taste 1 large garlic cloves, peeled and lightly crushed ◆ 1 handful (about ½ cup) Italian (flat-leaf) parsley, trimmed and chopped coarsely ◆ Parmesan shavings, to garnish

◆

1 Fill a large saucepan with water. Add 1 teaspoon salt. Bring to a boil over medium-high heat. Add the spaghetti and cook until al dente.

2 While the spaghetti is cooking, heat the olive oil in a large skillet over medium heat. Add the mushroom, rosemary, and garlic. Season with salt and pepper. Cook until the mushroom begins to soften (2 to 5 minutes). Remove from the heat.

3 Drain the spaghetti. Add to the mushroom mixture and the parsley. Toss well until the pasta is thoroughly coated in the sauce. Remove the rosemary, if desired.

4 Transfer to individual serving bowls and garnish with Parmesan shavings. Serve immediately.

Spaghetti with Cherry Tomatoes and Basil
Spaghetti al Pomodoro Cielegino e Basilico

*"Butta giu la pasta, Mama!"—"Throw in the pasta, Mom!" was the call from the boys
as we came back to the house for lunch, hungry and tired from working the fields. We
sat around the big, old table, chatting about the morning's work and tearing off hunks
of focaccia to satisfy our hunger. Mama had been preparing the food for most of the
morning. As the pasta arrived, our noisy banter was quickly replaced by the sounds
of slurping as we devoured the pasta. During these memorable lunches we often
feasted on Spaghetti al Pomodoro Cielegino e Basilico. A delicious blend of the fresh,
bittersweet cherry tomatoes of summer and the intense flavor of just-picked basil,
the dish was one of our all-time favorites.*

PREPARATION TIME: 10 minutes / **COOKING TIME:** 12 minutes / **SERVES:** 4

**1 handful (about ½ cup) basil leaves ◆ 2 pinches of salt ◆ 10 ounces uncooked spaghetti
¼ cup plus 1 tablespoon extra-virgin olive oil ◆ 1 medium red onion, chopped finely
1 small red chili, sliced thinly ◆ Pinch of freshly ground black pepper ◆ 20 cherry
tomatoes, halved ◆ 1 large garlic clove, lightly crushed by hand ◆ Parmesan cheese
(grated or shaved), to garnish**

◆

1 Tear the basil leaves into small pieces. Set aside.

2 Fill a large saucepan with water. Add a pinch of salt. Bring to a boil over medium-high heat. Place the spaghetti in the pot and boil until al dente.

3 While the spaghetti is cooking, heat the olive oil in a large skillet over medium-low heat. Add the onion and sauté until soft. Add the chili, pepper, and remaining salt. Stir to mix. Increase the heat to high and cook until sizzling hot (about 1 minute). Stir in the tomatoes and garlic. Sauté 3 minutes, stirring occasionally.

4 Drain the pasta. Place the pasta in the tomato mixture. Add the basil and toss until the pasta is coated in sauce. Transfer to large pasta bowls and top with grated or shaved Parmesan. Serve hot.

Butterfly Pasta with Ham and Fresh Peas
Farfalle ai Piselli Freschi con Prosciutto

We enjoyed the sweetness of peas in spring with this bow-tie pasta. It is a pretty and colorful dish, full of flavor, and now a favorite with our children, who love to help pod the peas. If you can't find fresh peas, the frozen, unminted variety is good, too.

PREPARATION TIME: 15 minutes / **COOKING TIME:** 12 minutes / **SERVES:** 4

2 teaspoons salt ◆ 1 cup fresh peas ◆ 10 ounces uncooked farfalle (bow-tie pasta)
¼ cup plus 1 tablespoon extra-virgin olive oil ◆ 1 medium yellow onion, chopped finely
3½ ounces prosciutto or cooked ham, chopped into ½-inch cubes ◆ 1 cup fresh peas
⅔ cup heavy cream ◆ Freshly ground black pepper to taste ◆ ½ cup grated Parmesan,
plus extra to garnish ◆ 1 handful fresh basil, torn into small pieces

◆

1 Fill a small saucepan with water. Add ½ teaspoon salt. Bring to a boil over medium-high heat. Add the peas and cook until just tender. Drain and set aside.

2 Fill a large saucepan with water. Add 1 teaspoon salt. Bring to a boil over medium-high heat. Add the farfalle and cook until al dente.

3 While the farfalle is cooking, heat the olive oil in a large skillet over medium-low heat. Add the onion and sauté until soft.

4 Add the peas, ham, cream, pepper, and remaining salt if necessary and cook for 1 to 2 minutes over a medium-low heat until all the ingredients are heated through.

5 Drain the pasta. Add to the pea mixture. Gently toss until the farfalle is well coated in sauce. Stir in the Parmesan and most of the basil.

6 Transfer to pasta bowls, garnish with extra Parmesan and the remaining basil, and serve.

Pasta with Forgotten Cheeses
Pasta ai Formaggi Dimenticati

This is a great way to use up any hard cheese that's left over from a meal or another recipe. My mother usually had leftover pecorino or Parmesan, and she'd always add a bit of dolcelatte to this dish to produce a bit more flavor. To make this recipe, we used milk straight from the cow, which was very creamy. These days, that type of milk is difficult to find, so I use heavy cream instead. This recipe is delicious and filling, so be hungry!

PREPARATION TIME: 5 minutes / **COOKING TIME:** 10 minutes / **SERVES:** 4

**Generous pinch of salt ◆ 10 ounces uncooked spaghetti, penne, or rigatoni
6 ounces hard cheese (any variety or combination of varieties)
⅔ cup heavy cream ◆ Freshly ground black pepper to taste
About 1 tablespoon grated Parmesan, to garnish**

◆

1 Fill a large saucepan with water. Add the salt and bring to a boil over medium-high heat.

2 Place the pasta in water and boil until al dente.

3 While the pasta is cooking, slice or crumble the cheese into small pieces and then place in a large saucepan.

4 Add the cream. Bring to a gentle simmer over low heat. Add pepper to taste. Simmer, stirring often, until the cheese is melted and the mixture is smooth.

5 Drain the pasta. Stir in the cheese mixture. Transfer to a serving bowl, garnish with Parmesan and, if desired, more pepper, and serve.

Rigatoni with White Meat Sauce
Rigatoni con Sugo Bianco

This has always been one of my favorite dishes. It's light and versatile, and it is one of the most frequently requested dishes in our restaurants. My mother had a food grinder attached to the table and we would grind up the cheaper cuts of meat.

PREPARATION TIME: 5 minutes / COOKING TIME: 20 minutes / SERVES: 4

¼ cup extra-virgin olive oil ◆ 1 medium white onion, chopped finely
1 pound boneless skinless chicken (or turkey or veal, or a combination), ground
1 large garlic clove, peeled and chopped finely ◆ 2 teaspoons salt ◆ 1 sprig fresh rosemary
Pinch of freshly ground black pepper ◆ ½ cup dry white wine ◆ 10 ounces uncooked
rigatoni or penne ◆ 1 tablespoon butter

◆

1 Heat the olive oil in a large skillet over medium-low heat. Add the onion and sauté until soft. Add the meat and cook, stirring constantly to avoid sticking, until browned.

2 Stir in the garlic, 1 teaspoon salt, rosemary, and pepper. Add the wine. Cook over medium-low heat for 15 to 20 minutes.

3 While the mixture is cooking, fill a large saucepan with water. Add the remaining salt and bring to a boil over medium-high heat. Place the rigatoni in the boiling water and cook until al dente. Drain.

4 Add the butter and rigatoni to the sauce and stir to mix. Transfer to a serving bowl. Serve with grated Parmesan. Remove rosemary before serving.

Baked Pasta with Tomato and Béchamel
Rigatoni Stracciati

My mother would make this as a way of using up leftover sauces—the quantities used were never the same, as it depended on what she had left. In this recipe I have used some roasted vegetables just as she often did. However, as a variation, you could omit these and use a quantity of Ragù (see page 94) instead of the tomato sauce.

PREPARATION TIME: 15 minutes / **COOKING TIME:** 20 to 25 minutes / **SERVES:** 6 to 8

Pinch of salt ◆ 2 cups Tomato Sauce (see page 89) ◆ 2 cups Béchamel (see page 90)
1 pound dried pasta such as rigotoni or penne ◆ 2 x 4½-ounce balls of mozzarella
10 ounces Roasted Vegetables (see page 39) ◆ ⅓ cup Parmesan, finely grated

◆

1 Pre-heat the oven to 350°F.

2 Fill a large saucepan with water and add the salt. Bring to a boil over medium-high heat. Put the pasta into the boiling water and cook until al dente.

3 While the pasta is cooking, put the tomato sauce and béchamel into a large pan over medium heat. Stir to combine and heat through.

4 Chop the mozzarella and roasted vegetables into bite-sized pieces.

5 Drain the pasta, then mix into the sauces. Add the chopped mozzarella and vegetables to the pasta and stir gently and briefly (stir too much and for too long and the cheese will begin to melt).

6 Pour the pasta into a large lasagne dish and scatter with the grated Parmesan. Bake in the over for about 20 to 25 minutes or until bubbling and golden brown.

Pappardelle with Rabbit and White Wine Ragù

Pappardelle con Ragù di Coniglio

We kept up to thirty rabbits in hutches at the back of our house. On Sundays or special occasions, one would end up on our table. This recipe uses two key ingredients in Tuscan cooking: soffritto, the foundation of many Tuscan dishes, and a good stock.

PREPARATION TIME: 20 minutes / **COOKING TIME:** 1 hour 10 minutes / **SERVES:** 4

⅓ **pound rabbit, cleaned** ◆ **3 cups uncooked Soffritto (see page 54)** ◆ **1 glass dry white wine** ◆ **1½ cups canned tomatoes, chopped** ◆ **1¼ cups Chicken Stock (see page 52)** **Salt to taste, plus 1 teaspoon extra for salting pasta water** ◆ **Freshly ground black pepper to taste** ◆ **12 ounces Fresh Long Pasta (see page 72)** ◆ **1 sprig rosemary, to garnish**

◆

1 Cut the rabbit into quarters and place in a large, heavy-bottomed saucepan. Add the raw Soffritto. Cook over medium heat, turning the rabbit occasionally, until browned on all sides.

2 Add the wine and cook, stirring frequently, for 10 minutes. Add the tomatoes and ¾ cup Chicken Stock. Increase the heat to medium-high and bring to a boil. Reduce the heat to medium-low and simmer 40 minutes, stirring occasionally, or until the meat comes away from the bones easily. (If necessary, add a bit more Chicken Stock to prevent drying.) Season with salt and pepper to taste.

3 Remove the pan from the heat. Remove the rabbit from the pan and place on a work surface. (Reserve the sauce in the pan.) Remove and discard the bones. Cut the meat into bite-sized pieces. Put the meat back into the sauce and stir to mix. Set aside.

4 Fill a large saucepan with water. Add the salt. Bring to a boil over medium-high heat. Place the pasta in the water and boil until al dente. Drain. Re-heat the sauce and add the drained pasta. Toss together to combine.

5 Transfer to pasta bowls. Garnish with rosemary and serve immediately.

Tuscan Pesto

Pesto alla Toscana

When I was a child, I knew of a pine tree near my friend Adriana's house. On the way home from school I would look for fallen pinecones and collect them. Adriana would get cross with me, as she wanted them for her family, but I would hurry away with them wrapped in my shirt. My mother, too, would scold me for stealing (and for my dirty clothes), but she was always pleased to use my treasure. The cones contained wonderful pine nuts—a highlight of this sauce.

PREPARATION TIME: 5 minutes / **COOKING TIME:** 0 minutes / **MAKES:** 2 cups

1 generous handful fresh basil, torn into small pieces
1 large garlic clove, peeled ◆ ½ cup pine nuts ◆ 1 cup extra-virgin olive oil
⅓ cup pecorino stagionato (hard) cheese, grated (available at specialty food stores)

◆

1 Place the basil, garlic, and pine nuts in a mortar. Crush together until the mixture is well blended, or use a food processor. Add the olive oil and cheese. Mix well and serve with any pasta.

2 Allow ¼ cup of pesto per person and store the remaining sauce in the refrigerator for up to 2 weeks. Make sure that the surface is always covered with olive oil.

Mama says:
Pesto is often served with spaghetti or penne—allow 1 cup of pasta per person and garnish with extra basil leaves.

Tomato Sauce for Pasta
Salsa di Pomodoro

My father used to store the summer's leftover tomatoes with basil and olive oil in airtight jars, for use throughout the fall. These days, we use canned tomatoes. I swear, though, that when I retire I will preserve my own.

PREPARATION TIME: 10 minutes / **COOKING TIME:** 30 minutes / **MAKES:** 3 cups

¼ cup plus 2 tablespoons extra-virgin olive oil
1 medium yellow onion, peeled and chopped finely
2 large garlic cloves, peeled and chopped finely ◆ Salt to taste
Freshly ground black pepper to taste ◆ 3⅓ cups diced tomatoes
1 handful fresh basil, torn into bite-sized pieces

◆

1 Heat the oil in a large saucepan over medium-low heat. Add the onion and sauté until soft. Stir in the garlic, salt, and pepper. Cook 2 minutes, stirring frequently.

2 Add the tomatoes, increasing the heat to medium-high, and bring to a boil.

3 Reduce the heat to low and simmer 30 minutes, until thickened. Adjust the seasonings, if desired. Stir in the basil. Serve with any pasta.

Béchamel

Colla Bianca

*Although this rich white sauce is associated with French cuisine, the delicacy
actually originated in Italy. Some say that the sauce was introduced to France
during the time of Catherine de Medici, in the early sixteenth century.
It is used today in lasagna and in countless other Italian dishes.*

PREPARATION TIME: 5 minutes / COOKING TIME: 15 minutes / MAKES: about 4¼ cups

4¼ cups whole milk ◆ **2 bay leaves** ◆ **1 medium white onion, peeled**
⅓ cup butter ◆ **⅓ cup all-purpose flour** ◆ **⅓ teaspoon freshly grated nutmeg**
Salt to taste ◆ **Pepper to taste**

◆

1 Place the milk, bay leaves, and onion in a
medium saucepan and bring to a boil over
medium heat.

2 While the milk is heating, melt the butter in
a medium saucepan over low heat. Whisk in the
flour, a little at a time, to make a roux or a
smooth paste.

3 Slowly add the boiled milk to the roux,
whisking constantly to produce a smooth sauce.
Add the nutmeg, salt, and pepper to taste. Leave
the onion and bay leaf in the sauce for flavor, but
remove before serving.

Mama says:
Use with Babbo's Pork and Beef Ragù
(see page 94) to make lasagna.

Butter and Mint Sauce
Salsa di Burro e Menta

This is a delicious sauce for filled pasta. It's particularly good on hot summer days—the mint is wonderfully refreshing and light. Prepare this sauce just before the pasta has finished cooking.

PREPARATION TIME: 2 minutes / **COOKING TIME:** 2 minutes / **SERVES:** 4

2 tablespoons butter ◆ ¼ cup pine nuts, toasted
8–10 fresh mint leaves, torn into small pieces
Freshly ground black pepper to taste

◆

1 Melt butter in a large skillet over low heat.

2 Add the pine nuts and mint. Add pepper to taste. Toss to mix.

Mama says:
Try whole sage leaves instead of mint for a classic "burreo salvia" sauce.

Hare Ragù

Ragù di Lepre

*Hares are abundant in Tuscany and were enjoyed in late winter or early spring.
The strong, gamey flavor is delicious in this sauce. It is a Tuscan favorite and is
usually served with freshly made pappardelle.*

PREPARATION TIME: 6 hours or more (to allow ingredients to marinate) plus 20 minutes
COOKING TIME: 1 hour / **SERVES:** 4

6- to 7-pound hare, cleaned and cut into quarters ◆ 1 bottle dry red wine
6 celery stalks, chopped coarsely ◆ 3 bay leaves ◆ 1 sprig fresh rosemary
4 large garlic cloves, peeled and left whole ◆ 1 medium yellow onion, peeled
and chopped coarsely ◆ 4 medium carrots, peeled and chopped coarsely
¼ cup plus 3 tablespoons extra-virgin olive oil ◆ 2¼ pounds tomatoes, skinned and
chopped coarsely ◆ 3 tablespoons tomato paste ◆ 1¾ cups hot Chicken or Vegetable Stock
(see pages 52 and 53) or water ◆ Salt to taste ◆ Freshly ground black pepper to taste

◆

1 Put the hare in a large pot. Add the wine, celery, bay leaves, rosemary, garlic, onion, and carrots. Cover and refrigerate 6 hours or overnight.

2 Place a large colander over a large bowl. Put the hare, vegetables, and marinade liquid in the colander. Separate the hare from the vegetables and set aside. Reserve the marinade liquid. Transfer the vegetables to a food processor and chop finely.

3 Heat the oil in a large saucepan over medium heat. Add the vegetables and sauté until soft (about 10 to 12 minutes). Add more oil if necessary, to prevent burning.

4 Add the hare to the vegetables. Brown the meat on all sides, turning often for about 15 minutes. Add the marinade, reduce the heat to medium-low, and cook for 5 minutes, stirring occasionally.

5 Add the tomatoes, tomato paste, and stock or water. Cook, stirring occasionally, until the meat comes away from the bone easily (about 1 hour). Add salt and pepper to taste.

6 Remove the hare from the pot. Discard the bones. Cut the meat into bite-sized pieces and put it back into the sauce. Cook 10 minutes, stirring occasionally. This dish can be stored for up to 1 week in a refrigerator.

Mama says:
Ask your butcher to bone the hare to save on preparation time and energy! This sauce tastes delicious served over a pasta of your choice.

Babbo's Pork and Beef Ragù
Ragù del Babbo

My father has been making this sauce for years. A basic yet delicious meat and tomato sauce, it is used in pici dishes, lasagna, and cannelloni. It will keep for up to 4 days in the refrigerator and can be frozen for up to 30 days. It tastes best served with either Fresh Pici (see page 69) or a short pasta such as penne.

PREPARATION TIME: 15 minutes / **COOKING TIME:** 1 hour / **SERVES:** 4

1½ cups cooked Soffritto, left in skillet (see page 54) ◆ 18 ounces ground pork
18 ounces ground beef ◆ ½ cup dry red wine
2¼ pounds canned tomatoes, skinned and chopped coarsely ◆ 1 sprig rosemary
3 cloves garlic ◆ Salt to taste ◆ Freshly ground black pepper to taste

◆

1 Add the pork and beef to the Soffritto. Stir to mix and cook over medium-low heat until the meat is browned (about 8 to 10 minutes).

2 Add the wine. Cook for 10 minutes, stirring occasionally.

3 Add the tomatoes, rosemary, and garlic. Season with salt and pepper to taste. Stir to mix. Reduce the heat to low and cook for 1 hour, stirring intermittently. Adjust seasonings, if desired.

Mama says:
This sauce may be served over any type of pasta.

Chapter four

Secondi
MAIN COURSES

Risotto Stuffed Peppers
Peperoni Ripieni con Risotto

This is a good way to use up leftover risotto, and the combination of sweet baked peppers and risotto is delicious. The peppers are tasty on their own, with tomato sauce, or as an accompaniment to grilled meat.

PREPARATION TIME: 5 minutes / **COOKING TIME:** 25 minutes / **SERVES:** 4

4 large red peppers
1½–2 cups (depending on size of peppers) Mushroom or Saffron Risotto (see page 64)
¾ cup grated pecorino or Parmesan, plus a little more for the tops of the peppers

◆

1 Preheat the oven to 350°F.

2 Slice off the tops of the peppers. Remove and discard the cores and seeds from the peppers.

3 Mix the risotto with the cheese in a bowl, then stuff the peppers.

4 Transfer the peppers to a baking tray and scatter over the remaining cheese. Place tops of the peppers on risotto and cheese.

5 Bake for 25 minutes or until the peppers are soft and the risotto is piping hot.

Mama says:
Red peppers tend to be sweeter than green ones, so they are ideal for stuffing. Choose peppers that are glossy and firm. Make sure the flesh is thick and that the skin is not marked.

Frittata of Peas and Zucchini
Frittata di Piselli e Zucchine

Mama used to make frittatas when she wanted a quick meal. They usually contained seasonal vegetables, and sometimes potatoes as well. Sometimes they contained just chives, basil, or mint. We make frittatas at our restaurant every day, and they're always a big hit. Serve this with a crisp salad of seasonal greens.

PREPARATION TIME: 30 minutes / COOKING TIME: 12 to 15 minutes / SERVES: 4

About 1½ teaspoons salt ◆ 1¼ cups fresh peas ◆ ¼ cup extra-virgin olive oil
1 medium yellow onion, chopped finely
2 medium zucchini, sliced thinly
Freshly ground black pepper to taste ◆ 6 large eggs

◆

1 Fill a medium saucepan with water. Add 1 teaspoon salt. Bring to a boil over medium-high heat. Add the peas and boil until just tender (about 5 minutes, but test them frequently, as the cooking time depends on their size). Drain.

2 While the peas are cooking, heat the olive oil in a large skillet over medium heat. Add the onion and sauté until soft. Add the zucchini. Season with salt and pepper to taste. Fry until the zucchini is lightly browned and tender (about 2 to 5 minutes).

3 While the zucchini is cooking, place the eggs in a medium bowl. Season with salt and pepper to taste and beat lightly. Set aside.

4 Add the peas to the zucchini-onion mixture. Stir. Pour in the eggs (do not stir) and cook for 4 to 5 minutes or until the eggs are cooked. Make sure that the mixture doesn't burn.

5 Place a serving plate upside down over the frittata. Holding the plate firmly in place, invert the skillet and plate so that the frittata falls onto the plate.

6 Slide the frittata back into the skillet for a couple of minutes to cook the underside.

7 When cooked, slide the frittata onto a serving plate and serve at room temperature in wedges or chopped into small squares of antipasti.

Swallows' Nests

Nidi di Rondine

We had swallows' nests under the eaves of our house. The swallows returned every year, bringing with them good luck. We honored their return by making these nests filled with eggs. As children, my brother and I used to love helping Mama prepare this dish. It was delicious and fun to eat. The dough is made from flour, potatoes, and eggs—similar to gnocchi. Today, we can purchase potatoes at any time of the year, but that was not the case for my family when I was growing up. We kept our season's harvest of potatoes stored in a hollowed-out bank covered with straw, burlap, and earth. This prevented the frost (and animals) from attacking our supply. In this way our potatoes lasted throughout the long winter months.

PREPARATION TIME: 40 minutes / **COOKING TIME:** 8 minutes / **SERVES:** 4

**18 ounces potatoes, unpeeled ◆ 1 large egg, beaten ◆ Salt to taste
Freshly ground black pepper to taste ◆ 1 cup all-purpose flour ◆ 4–5 tablespoons olive oil
4 eggs ◆ Grated Parmesan cheese to serve ◆ Fresh basil leaves to garnish**

◆

1 Place the potatoes in a large saucepan. Cover with water and bring to a boil over medium-high heat. Boil until soft, then drain off the water, set the potatoes aside, and rinse the pan.

2 Peel the potatoes. Return to the pan. Add the eggs and mash to mix thoroughly. Season with salt and pepper to taste.

3 Gradually add flour, a tablespoon at a time, mashing after each addition. Transfer the mixture to a work surface and knead until the texture is firm but flexible.

4 Shape the mixture into round, 2½-inch-diameter "nests."

5 Heat the oil in a large skillet over medium heat. Add the nests in batches. Fry until golden brown on the bottoms. Gently turn and fry until the tops of the nests are golden brown. Remove from the pan and drain on paper towels before serving.

6 Fill nests with Tomato Sauce (see page 89), fried eggs, or both. Sprinkle with Parmesan and garnish with fresh basil.

Eel Cooked with Tomatoes
Anguille in Umido

In the marshland around our house were many streams and ponds; by diverting the water from a pond we often found nests of eels in the mud. With our hands wrapped in burlap to keep the eels from slipping through our hands, we caught the eels and cooked them. This dish is particularly good accompanied by roasted potatoes.

PREPARATION TIME: 10 minutes / **COOKING TIME:** 50 minutes / **SERVES:** 4

2 cups plus 1 tablespoon extra-virgin olive oil ◆ 1 yellow onion, chopped finely
3 cloves garlic, crushed by hand ◆ 1 medium-sized eel, cleaned and gutted
½ cup dry white wine ◆ 1 teaspoon salt ◆ Freshly ground black pepper to taste
3⅓ cups diced tomatoes

---

1 Heat the olive oil in a large skillet over medium heat. Add the onion and garlic and sauté until the onion is soft (about 5 minutes).

2 Increase the heat to medium-high. Add the eel and sear on all sides (about 2 minutes).

3 Reduce the heat to medium-low. Add the wine, salt, and pepper. Cook for 3 minutes.

4 Reduce the heat to low, stir in the tomatoes, and simmer for 30 to 40 minutes or until the eel is tender.

Pike Baked in a Terra-cotta Dish
Luccio al Tegame

A tegame is a large, round terra-cotta pot with a cover. It has to be good quality, preferably made in Italy. The bakeware gives great flavor to the food. Bad terra-cotta leaves a smell on the food. If no high-quality terra-cotta dish is available, use a good casserole dish with a lid. Once or twice a month, the fish merchant came to our house to sell my mother seafood. My first memories of him were on a bicycle, with a small trailer attached to the bicycle's back. Later, he drove a moped, with a box strapped on behind him. He caught his bounty in the canals near our house, and he usually had pike, perch, or eel. If we suspected that his fish were old, we sent him packing, but he always came back the next month.

PREPARATION TIME: 10 minutes / **COOKING TIME:** 50 minutes / **SERVES:** 4

1 cup all-purpose flour ◆ Pinch of salt ◆ Pinch of freshly ground black pepper 4 tablespoons extra-virgin olive oil ◆ 2- to 3-pound pike or similar firm, white-fleshed fish, cleaned and scaled ◆ 4 large garlic cloves, unpeeled ◆ 3 bay leaves 2 cups cooked Soffritto (see page 54), prepared and left in a tegame or covered casserole dish ◆ 14 ounces canned tomatoes, chopped but not drained 1 tablespoon capers, washed and drained (the small, salted variety has the best flavor)

◆

1 In a medium bowl, mix together the flour, salt, and pepper.

2 Heat the oil in a large skillet over medium heat. While the oil is heating, cut the pike into four large pieces. Spread the flour onto a large plate and coat the pieces in the flour mixture.

3 Place the pike in the skillet and fry 3 minutes on both sides, until golden brown.

4 Add the garlic cloves and bay leaves to the Soffritto. Lay the pike on the Soffritto in the *tegame*. Top with the tomatoes and capers.

5 Cover the *tegame*. Bake in the oven for 35 to 40 minutes or until the pike is cooked through.

6 Serve straight from the *tegame* or transfer to a serving platter and serve with Sautéed Spinach (see page 36) or potatoes of your choice.

Perch in Bread Crumbs
Persico al Forno con Molliche di Pane

We occasionally caught perch from the river near our house for this recipe; however, various other fleshy white fish such as sea bream. In the summer, we cooked this outside on the grill—nowadays you can use a barbecue. It takes around the same amount of time to bake the fish in a baking pan covered with foil. In winter, we used a mixture of herbs such as rosemary, thyme, and a whole bay leaf, but in summer we tended to use milder herbs such as basil, tarragon, and parsley. This dish is delicious served with a fresh salad and crusty bread to mop up the juices.

PREPARATION TIME: 20 minutes / **COOKING TIME:** 20 to 30 minutes
SERVES: 4 to 6, depending on the size of the fish

2 cups white bread crumbs ◆ **3 large garlic cloves, peeled and chopped finely**
2 teaspoons tarragon, roughly chopped ◆ **2 teaspoons parsley**
2 teaspoons thyme ◆ **Salt to taste** ◆ **Freshly ground black pepper to taste**
2- to 3-pound perch or similar white-fleshed fish, deboned and washed
3 tablespoons extra-virgin olive oil

◆

1 Preheat the oven to 375°F.

2 Place the bread crumbs, garlic, tarragon, parsley, thyme, salt, and pepper in a medium bowl. Using your hands, mix well.

3 Ask your butcher to bone the fish, but leave it together at the top and open along the bottom.

Stuff the cavity with the bread crumb mixture, along the entire length of the fish.

4 Lightly grease a baking dish. Place the fish in the dish and drizzle with olive oil.

5 Bake for 20 to 30 minutes or until the fish is cooked through.

Salt Cod Baked in Tomatoes and Onion
Baccala in Umido

Dried cod, or salt cod, keeps for ages, but it must be washed in water to remove the salt and soaked in water for 24 hours in the refrigerator before it is used in order to rehydrate the fish and remove the salt. The soaking water should be changed three times during the day.

PREPARATION TIME: 24 hours (to allow cod to soak) plus 10 minutes
COOKING TIME: 35 minutes / **SERVES:** 4

About ¾ cup extra-virgin olive oil ◆ 1 side of cod, dried (not sold by weight)
About 1 cup all-purpose flour, for dusting ◆ 1 large egg, lightly beaten
2 medium yellow onions, peeled and chopped finely ◆ 3 large garlic cloves, peeled
Salt to taste ◆ Freshly ground black pepper to taste
16 to 18 ounces canned diced tomatoes

◆

1 Preheat the oven to 375°F. Heat ½ cup olive oil in a large skillet over medium heat.

2 While the oil is heating, cut the cod into four pieces. Spread the flour out onto a large plate and pour the beaten egg into a shallow dish. Lightly coat the cod pieces in flour, then dip into the egg.

3 Place the cod in the skillet and fry until golden brown on both sides. Remove from the skillet and set aside. Discard the oil and clean the skillet.

4 Heat the remaining oil in the skillet, and when hot, add the onions and garlic. Season with salt and pepper, to taste. Sauté until the onions are soft and then stir in the tomatoes.

5 Transfer the mixture to a baking dish. Place the cod over the mixture. Bake for 20 minutes or until the cod is cooked and the pan juices have reduced.

6 Transfer to a serving plate and serve with vegetables or potatoes of your choice.

Mustard Chicken

Pollo alla Senape

This dish calls for strong, hot mustard that, once cooked, has a flavor that is quite mild. In the UK we use English mustard, which may be purchased in specialty food stores and in some grocery stores. Coleman's is a good brand to choose. It's bright yellow in color and can be bought prepared or as a dry powder; follow the manufacturer's instructions for making it into a paste.

PREPARATION TIME: 10 minutes / **COOKING TIME:** 60 to 70 minutes / **SERVES:** 4

4 medium red onions, peeled and sliced into rings ◆ Salt to taste
Freshly ground black pepper to taste ◆ 4½-pound whole chicken, cut in half
(ask your butcher to prepare this for you if you don't have a good enough knife)
½ cup English mustard ◆ ¼ cup extra-virgin olive oil ◆ ½ cup dry white wine

◆

1 Preheat the oven to 375°F.

2 Place the onions in a baking dish in a single layer. Season with salt and pepper to taste.

3 Cut the chicken in half. Add salt and pepper to taste. Spread the mustard over the chicken, pushing it into the crevices and making sure the surface is well covered.

4 Lay the chicken pieces over the onions, pour the oil on top, and bake for 30 minutes. Add the wine and bake the chicken for 30 to 40 minutes more or until the juices run clear when poked with a skewer. Serve on plates with the onions and sauce poured on top.

Mama says:
Don't be shy about using a lot of mustard—you'll be amazed at how the strength of the flavor dissipates during cooking.

Chicken with Pinenuts and Raisins

Pollo Lesso Rifatto

When the older hens stopped laying eggs, we used them to make stock. If a hen is not available for this dish, a capon can be used instead. The older the hen, the tougher the meat, which means that it can withstand the long boiling time and will retain a good flavor.

PREPARATION TIME: 15 minutes / **COOKING TIME:** 2 hours 40 minutes / **SERVES:** 4

4½-pound whole hen or capon (ask your butcher for an older bird, for more flavor)
2 medium carrots, whole ◆ 2 celery stalks ◆ 1 medium yellow onion, peeled ◆ Salt to taste
Freshly ground black pepper to taste ◆ 3 tablespoons extra-virgin olive oil
⅓ cup stock ◆ 1 cup pine nuts ◆ 1 cup golden raisins

◆

1 Place the hen in a large saucepan. Add the carrots, celery, onion, and salt. Cover with water and bring to a boil over medium-high heat. Boil until the hen is cooked through and the meat comes away easily from the bone (2 to 2½ hours). Remove from the heat.

2 Transfer the hen to a work surface and reserve the stock (you can freeze any left over for use in another recipe.) Remove the meat from the bone, leaving the skin on larger pieces of flesh. Discard the bones.

3 Season the meat with salt and pepper.

4 Heat the olive oil in a large skillet over medium-high heat. Add the meat. Fry until crispy (about 5 minutes either side), turning occasionally.

5 Stir in the stock, pine nuts, and raisins. Transfer to a serving platter. Pour the pan juices over the meat and serve immediately with Potato-Parmesan Mash (see page 43) or Roasted Vegetables (see page 39).

Roasted Chicken and Guinea Fowl with Vegetables

Arrosto Misto

I consider this my "signature dish." I love to make it because it is simple, yet full of flavor. My mother made it with a mixture of these meats and often with chicken on its own. Now we teach this in our cooking schools, and it is one of those recipes that customers tell us they have cooked repeatedly. Use any vegetables you like—we sometimes add parsnips and mushrooms.

PREPARATION TIME: 30 minutes / **COOKING TIME:** 1 hour 30 minutes / **SERVES:** 6

5 cloves of garlic, unpeeled and lightly crushed by hand ◆ 1 bunch (3 ounces) fresh sage leaves ◆ 3 sprigs fresh rosemary, trimmed ◆ 2 tablespoons salt
2 tablespoons freshly ground black pepper ◆ 4-pound whole chicken, cut in half
3-pound guinea fowl, cut in half ◆ 4 medium carrots, trimmed, peeled, and cut into 1-inch-long pieces ◆ 4 small zucchini, trimmed and cut into 1-inch-long pieces ◆ 3 sweet potatoes, cut into 1-inch cubes ◆ ½ cup extra-virgin olive oil

◆

1 Preheat the oven to 400°F. Finely chop the garlic, sage, and rosemary. Place together in a small bowl. Add salt and pepper and mix well.

2 Cut small slits all over the chicken and guinea fowl. Stuff the herb mixture into the slits.

3 Place the meat, carrots, zucchini, potatoes, and oil in a large terra-cotta baking dish or a roasting pan. Generously sprinkle with salt and pepper. Bake for about 1–1½ hours or until the juices run clear and the vegetables are lightly browned.

4 Remove the dish from the oven. Transfer the meat to a cutting board. Cut into individual portions for six people. Arrange the vegetables in the dish in a single layer. Place the meat on top of the vegetables. Return to the oven and bake 5 minutes more.

5 Remove the dish from the oven. Let rest for 10 minutes before serving. Serve in the terra-cotta baking dish or roasting pan or carefully transfer to a serving platter.

Stuffed Chicken

Pollo Ripieno

Poor families such as ours made use of any stale bread, avoiding wastage and adding more bulk to the chicken dish to fill hungry boys' stomachs. Herbs were available fresh from Babbo's garden and made a delicious and succulent stuffing that tasted good on its own, imparted a wonderful flavor to the chicken as a whole, and kept the bird nice and moist while it was cooking in the oven. This recipe can be stored in the refrigerator for 2 or 3 days and eaten cold, but it is most enjoyable served immediately, with potatoes and vegetables of your choice.

PREPARATION TIME: 40 minutes / **COOKING TIME:** 60 to 75 minutes / **SERVES:** 4

4½-pound whole chicken, deboned (ask your butcher to prepare this; leave the skin on)
Salt to taste ◆ Freshly ground black pepper to taste ◆ 2 celery stalks, cut into large chunks
2 medium carrots, cut into large chunks ◆ ¾ pound potatoes, peeled and cut into halves
¼ cup plus 1 tablespoon extra-virgin olive oil ◆ 1 sprig rosemary

STUFFING
2 cups Tuscan or other farmhouse-style white bread
1 small yellow onion, chopped finely
1 handful Italian (flat-leaf) parsley, chopped finely ◆ 6 sage leaves, chopped finely
2 sprigs oregano, chopped finely
2 large garlic cloves, peeled and chopped finely ◆ 1 large egg, lightly beaten

◆

1 Preheat the oven to 375°F.

2 Spread the chicken flat, skin side down, on a work surface. Season with salt and pepper. Set aside.

3 Place the bread in a large bowl of water and let it soak 30 seconds. Remove the bread from the water and squeeze out excess water. (The bread should be spongy, not soggy.) Rinse and dry the bowl.

4 Tear the bread into small pieces and place in the bowl. Add the onion, parsley, sage, oregano, garlic, and egg. Season with salt and pepper to taste. Mix well using your hands.

5 Shape the stuffing into a ball and fill the cavity of the chicken. Wrap the chicken around the stuffed cavity, making sure that the skin covers all of the flesh. Secure tightly with kitchen string. Wrap the string around the chicken in several places to keep the bird secure while cooking.

6 Place the chicken in a roasting pan. Arrange the celery, carrots, and potatoes around the chicken. Season with salt and pepper. Pour the oil over all the ingredients. Add the rosemary.

7 Bake until the chicken is cooked and the juices run clear (60 to 75 minutes).

8 Transfer to a serving platter, remove the string, discard the rosemary, and serve.

Mama says:
Why not try making up your own stuffing? A combination of pine nuts, rice, and golden raisins would work just as well as the stuffing in this recipe.

Partridge and Vin Santo
Pernice al Vin Santo

My uncle caught birds by leaving traps made from cow tail hairs. When he got lucky we could share in his bounty and my father would bring out his home-made Vin Santo made from semi-dried grapes.

PREPARATION TIME: 10 minutes **COOKING TIME:** 35 minutes / **SERVES:** 4

4 partridge ◆ 4 slices of pancetta or bacon ◆ 4 sprigs fresh rosemary
4 bay leaves ◆ Salt and freshly ground pepper to taste ◆ ⅓ cup extra-virgin olive oil
◆ ⅓ cup Vin Santo ◆ Chicken Stock (about 1 cup) (see page 52)

◆

1 Preheat the oven to 350°F.

2 Take a slice of pancetta and place 1 sprig rosemary and 1 bay leaf at one end and roll up. Place the pancetta roll inside one partridge, then repeat with the others.

3 Place the partridges in a baking dish, drizzle with half the olive oil, and put them in the pre-heated oven. Cook for 15 to 20 minutes, or until the juices run clear but the partridges are only just done. Remove from the oven.

4 Heat the remaining olive oil in a large skillet over medium heat. When hot add the partridges and any juices from the baking dish. Turn as required to crispen the skin.

5 Pour in the Vin Santo and reduce for a couple of minutes. Add a few spoonfuls of stock to increase the amount of liquid for the sauce, then reduce again.

6 Serve immediately, finished with the sauce drizzled over the tops. As a side dish, mashed potato and black kale tastes great.

Roasted Squab with Bacon
Piccione Arrosto con Lardo

Squabs were rare treats when I was a child, but we were sometimes able to catch them. Today, squabs are available for purchase at specialty food stores. In this recipe, bacon adds flavor to the bird and prevents it from becoming dry while baking. Serve this dish with roasted potatoes and vegetables.

PREPARATION TIME: 10 minutes / **COOKING TIME:** 35 minutes / **SERVES:** 2

**6 fresh sage leaves ◆ 1 sprig fresh rosemary, whole ◆ 2 whole cloves garlic, lightly crushed
2 squabs, cleaned ◆ Salt to taste ◆ Freshly ground black pepper to taste
10 strips bacon ◆ ½ cup dry red wine**

◆

1 Preheat the oven to 375°F. Place about half of the sage, rosemary, and garlic inside the squab cavities. Season the cavities with salt and pepper. Rub the remaining rosemary and sage onto the squabs, then season to taste.

2 Wrap the squabs in bacon and place in a baking dish.

3 Cover and bake for 20 minutes. Add the wine. Bake for another 15 minutes or until the squabs are cooked through and the juices have reduced.

4 Transfer the squabs to a serving platter. Spoon the juices over the squabs and serve.

Pork Liver

Fegato di Maiale

Mama always prepared this dish in November, just after the year's pig had been killed. Most parts of the pig could be preserved in some way, but the liver had to be eaten immediately. My brother and I loved it, and I still enjoy it today. This goes very well with mashed potatoes.

PREPARATION TIME: 5 minutes / **COOKING TIME:** 2 minutes / **SERVES:** 4

3 tablespoons extra-virgin olive oil ◆ 1-pound pork liver
All-purpose flour, for coating ◆ Salt to taste ◆ Freshly ground black pepper to taste
3 tablespoons butter ◆ 4 fresh sage leaves

◆

1 Heat the olive oil in a large skillet over medium heat.

2 While the oil is heating, cut the liver into thin slices, about three slices per person.

3 In a medium bowl, mix together the flour, salt, and pepper. Lightly coat the liver in the flour mixture.

4 Place the liver in the skillet. Cook 1 minute. Flip the liver and cook 1 minute more or until cooked to taste.

5 Place the butter and sage leaves in the skillet. Shake the pan to blend the flavors. Transfer the liver to a serving plate. Serve with the sage leaves and butter poured over the top.

Baked Pork Loin with Quinces

Lombata di Maiale al Forno con Mele Cotogne

When choosing quinces for this recipe, pick larger varieties with a smooth surface.
You can store quinces for several months.

PREPARATION TIME: 30 minutes / **COOKING TIME:** 1 hour / **SERVES:** 4

2¼-pound pork loin, deboned (or leave bone in and carve yourself) ◆ Salt to taste
Freshly ground black pepper to taste ◆ 1 sprig fresh rosemary, chopped finely
5 large garlic cloves, peeled and sliced ◆ 6 ripe quinces, quartered
4 tablespoons brown sugar ◆ Extra-virgin olive oil, to drizzle

◆

1 Preheat the oven to 375°F.

2 Cut several shallow slits in the pork. Push the salt, pepper, rosemary, and garlic into the slits. Generously sprinkle salt and pepper over the pork.

3 Transfer the pork to a baking dish. Place the quinces around the pork. Sprinkle sugar over the quinces.

4 Drizzle oil over the pork and quinces. Bake for 1 hour or until the pork is cooked through but still tender.

5 Transfer the pork and its juices to a serving plate and serve with a potato dish such as garlic Potato-Parmesan Mash (see page 43).

Pork Ribs

Costoleccio di Maiale

When a pig was killed, we preserved some of the ribs with salt and vinegar. They
would keep for up to a month. Others were eaten fresh and grilled plain.
Serve with crusty bread and salad or Roasted Vegetables (see page 39.)

PREPARATION TIME: 5 minutes / **COOKING TIME:** 10 to 15 minutes if grilled, 30 minutes if baked /
SERVES: 4

2 tablespoons olive oil ◆ 1 large garlic clove, finely chopped
Salt to taste ◆ Freshly ground black pepper to taste ◆ 1¼ pounds whole pork ribs

◆

1 If using an oven rather than a grill, preheat
to 375°F. Rub the olive oil, garlic, salt, and
pepper onto the ribs. Place the ribs on the grill
or bake in a roasting pan in the oven.

2 The meat is cooked when it comes away from
the bone easily. It should be brown rather than
pink. At this point, flip and cook the other side
of the ribs, whichever cooking method you use.

Pork Chops with Pecorino and Spinach
Costoletta di Maiale con Pecorino e Spinaci

*Spinach is commonly used in Tuscan cookery, as it grows easily in our climate.
My mother used it in many ways from stuffing pasta to accompanying meat, and
even in sweet tart with pinenuts and raisins. Pecorino is the local sheep's cheese
and is used frequently instead of Parmesan.*

PREPARATION TIME: 5 minutes / **COOKING TIME:** 16 minutes / **SERVES:** 4

4 pork chops (approximately 5 ounces each) ◆ 3 ounces pecorino cheese
3 ounces cooked spinach, squeezed thoroughly ◆ Salt and freshly ground pepper to taste
½ cup all-purpose flour ◆ 7 tablespoons extra-virgin olive oil ◆ ⅔ cup white wine
Scant 1 cup meat stock, warmed ◆ 5 tablespoons butter ◆ 12 sage leaves ◆ 4 garlic cloves

◆

1 Make a 1-inch horizontal cut into the wide
end of each pork chop. Push the knife inside,
taking care not to break through either the top
or the bottom edges, and slide it back and forth
to create a pocket.

2 Cut the pecorino cheese in quarters and
divide the cooked spinach into 4 portions. Put
1 piece of cheese and 1 portion of spinach inside
each pocket, then squeeze the opening shut
between your fingers. Season all sides of the pork
chop with salt and pepper, to taste, then dredge
with flour.

3 Heat the oil in a large skillet over medium-
high heat. When hot, sear the chops on all sides
including the fatty edge. When browned all over
reduce to medium heat and pour in the wine.
Reduce the liquid for a few minutes.

4 Pour in the warmed stock, then add the
butter, sage leaves, and garlic cloves (skins on
but lightly crushed). Cook for 5 to 10 minutes,
or until the pork chops are cooked through.
Baste them frequently with the juices from the
pan, and halfway through the cooking time, turn
the chops over.

5 Serve each pork chop on a bed of mashed
potato, if liked, and cooked spinach. Drizzle
over the sauce and garnish with a couple of
sage leaves.

Pork Sausages Baked with Tomatoes
Salsicce di Maiale in Umido

My mother made lovely sausages by stuffing ground pork into the skin from the guts. Now we buy Tuscan sausages from our butcher. They are short and thick and have a low fat content. Buy the best quality sausages you can find, without any added flavorings, to produce a truly delicious dish.

PREPARATION TIME: 30 minutes / **COOKING TIME:** 50 minutes / **SERVES:** 4

8 pork sausages ◆ 1 cup cooked Soffritto (see page 54), still in the pan
2 tablespoons dry white wine ◆ 14 ounces canned plum tomatoes, chopped coarsely
2 tablespoons extra-virgin olive oil ◆ Salt to taste ◆ Freshly ground black pepper to taste

1 Place the sausages in a skillet and fry over medium heat until golden brown (4 to 5 minutes).

2 Place the sausages in the skillet with the Soffritto. Add the wine. Simmer over low heat, 2 minutes, until the wine has reduced.

3 Add the tomatoes and olive oil; season to taste with salt and pepper. Simmer 30 minutes. Transfer to a serving plate and serve hot with a potato dish such as garlic roasted potatoes.

Sausages with Peas and Tomatoes
Salsicce ai Piselli e Pomodori

We ate sausages quite often as children, so we had a variety of sausage dishes to enjoy. In this recipe, the peas sweeten the dish. In the summer we used fresh peas and in the winter we used canned.

PREPARATION TIME: 10 minutes / **COOKING TIME:** 35 minutes / **SERVES:** 4

1 teaspoon salt, plus extra to taste ◆ 1¼ cups fresh peas
¼ cup plus 1 tablespoon extra-virgin olive oil ◆ 1 cup finely chopped yellow onion
8 Italian pork sausages ◆ Freshly ground black pepper
14 ounces canned tomatoes

◆

1 Fill a medium saucepan with water. Add 1 teaspoon salt. Bring to a boil over medium-high heat. Add the peas and cook until just tender (about 5 minutes). Drain.

2 Heat the olive oil in a large skillet over medium heat. Add the onion and sauté until soft (2 to 5 minutes).

3 Place the sausages in the skillet. Add salt and pepper to taste (do not oversalt—sausage may already be salty). Cook, turning frequently, until the sausages are browned on all sides (about 7 minutes). Add the tomatoes and heat through.

4 When the sausages have cooked (about 10 minutes), add the peas and serve immediately.

Skewered Meatballs Wrapped in Pancetta with Mozzarella

Speidini di Fegatelli Falsi

As children we used to eat fegatelli, which were little parcels of pig's liver wrapped in caul and cooked in lard. However, with today's change in taste and availability of offal, we have adapted the recipe to suit our children's taste. For them, we have included a surprise inside the parcels of a morsel of oozing mozzarella.

PREPARATION TIME: 20 minutes / **COOKING TIME:** 10 to 15 minutes / **SERVES:** 4

3½ ounces white bread from an unsliced loaf, torn into small chunks
2 big sprigs of parsley, thick stalks removed ◆ 1 clove garlic ◆ 1 pound ground beef
1 egg ◆ ¼ cup fresh Parmesan ◆ Salt and freshly ground pepper to taste
2½ ounces mozzarella, cut into bite-size cubes ◆ 6 strips thinly sliced pancetta
or sliced bacon ◆ 12 bay leaves ◆ 1 tablespoon extra-virgin olive oil

◆

1 Soak four wooden skewers in water for at least 20 minutes before cooking.

2 Pre-heat the grill to high.

3 Put the bread, parsley, and garlic into a food processor and whiz to make fine crumbs. Combine with the ground beef and egg in a large bowl. Season to taste.

4 Divide the mixture into about 16 portions weighing approximately ¼ ounces each. Mold each portion into a ball-shape and push a piece of mozzarella into the center. Close up the opening and wrap each ball in a strip of Pancetta.

5 Thread four balls onto the wooden skewers separating each portion with a bay leaf. Brush with a little oil and put under the grill to cook, turning the skewers over half way through cooking. They should take 10 to 15 minutes. Serve warm with crusty bread and dressed salad leaves.

Pig's Foot

Zampone di Maiale

Pig's foot was a popular treat when I was a child. In Italy, offal is called cucina povera, *meaning "poor food," as these were the cuts of the pig that agrarian Italians would eat so as not to waste any meat. Offal is still very popular all over Europe today.*

PREPARATION TIME: 40 minutes / **COOKING TIME:** 50 minutes / **SERVES:** 4

5 cups Chicken Stock (see page 52) ◆ 1 medium-sized pig's foot
14 ounces ground veal ◆ 2 cups bread crumbs ◆ 1 yellow onion, chopped finely
1 large garlic clove, peeled and chopped finely ◆ Salt to taste
Freshly ground black pepper to taste ◆ Cayenne pepper to taste
1 small bunch (about 1 ounce) Italian (flat-leaf) parsley, chopped coarsely
1 large egg, lightly beaten

◆

1 Place the stock in a large saucepan that has a tight-fitting lid. Bring the stock to a boil over medium heat.

2 Using a sharp knife, cut down one side of the pig's foot and around the bone, separating the meat from the bone. Set the meat aside. Discard the bone.

3 In a large bowl, mix together the veal, bread crumbs, onion, garlic, salt, black pepper, cayenne pepper, parsley, and egg. Stuff the mixture into the pig's foot. Using kitchen string, secure the pig's foot.

4 Place the pig's foot in the stock. Cover the saucepan and simmer over medium-low heat for 50 to 60 minutes.

5 Transfer the pig's foot to a serving platter, slice with a carving knife, and serve.

Beef Stewed with Black Peppercorns and Tomatoes

Peposo

According to my grandfather, Nonno, the workers at the brick factories used the furnaces there to make this delicious stew, using the cheap stewing steak that was available to the poor. The secret to this delicious dish is slow cooking, which can take up to four hours. After that length of time, the meat melts in the mouth and the sharp heat of the peppercorns is mellowed to a warm glow. Put Peposo into the oven on a Sunday morning and enjoy it that evening with an earthy wine such as Brunello di Montalcino. This is now one of the signature dishes at our restaurant.

PREPARATION TIME: 5 minutes / **COOKING TIME:** 4 hours / **SERVES:** 4

2¼ pounds chuck roast, chopped into 1½-inch cubes ◆ 8 cups cold water
6 large garlic cloves, peeled and left whole ◆ ¼ cup black peppercorns ◆ 10 bay leaves
1 teaspoon salt ◆ 14 ounces canned whole tomatoes

---

1 Place the meat and water in a large saucepan. Add the garlic, peppercorns, bay leaves, and salt. Bring to a boil over medium-high heat. Reduce the heat to low and simmer for 1 hour.

2 Add the tomatoes. Simmer for 2 to 3 hours, until the beef is tender, stirring occasionally. If necessary, add a little water to prevent the beef from drying. Once the meat is tender, serve with polenta or rice.

Roasted Rabbit, Dead

Arrosto Morto di Coniglio

Despite its strange name, this is a delicious roast. The "dead" in the recipe's name refers to the simplicity—the "plainness"—of the dish by Tuscan standards. This recipe may be used to cook almost any type of meat (although cooking times will vary). Serve this with garlic roast potatoes.

PREPARATION TIME: 5 minutes / **COOKING TIME:** 1 hour / **SERVES:** 4

3-pound rabbit, cleaned ◆ **¼ cup plus 1 tablespoon extra-virgin olive oil**
6 large garlic cloves, unpeeled ◆ **2 sprigs fresh rosemary, chopped finely**
Salt to taste ◆ **Freshly ground black pepper to taste** ◆ **½ cup dry white wine**

◆

1 Preheat the oven to 400°F.

2 Cut the rabbit into large pieces. Place in a baking dish.

3 In a medium bowl, mix together the olive oil, garlic, rosemary, salt, and pepper. Pour over the rabbit and toss to coat.

4 Bake for 25 to 30 minutes.

5 Pour the wine over the rabbit. Baste the rabbit in the wine and pan juices. Bake for another 30 to 35 minutes or until the meat is cooked and comes away from the bone easily.

6 Transfer the rabbit to a serving platter. Pour the pan juices into a gravy boat. Serve. The garlic cloves will soften during cooking—their insides become pastelike and can be squeezed out with the back of a knife and enjoyed as a condiment.

Rabbit Cooked in Terra-cotta

Coniglio al Tegame

We ate rabbit fairly often and this dish was very easy for my mother to prepare. Use a casserole dish with a lid, preferably made of good Italian terra-cotta

PREPARATION TIME: 20 minutes / **COOKING TIME:** 50 to 60 minutes / **SERVES:** 4

5¼- to 6¼-pound rabbit, skinned and cleaned ◆ 3 large garlic cloves, unpeeled
3 sprigs fresh rosemary ◆ ¼ cup plus 2 tablespoons olive oil ◆ Salt to taste
Freshly ground black pepper to taste ◆ 6 large potatoes, peeled and chopped
into 1-inch chunks ◆ ½ cup dry white wine

◆

1 Preheat the oven to 400°F.

2 Cut the rabbit into large pieces and place in a terra-cotta baking dish. Add garlic and rosemary. Pour the olive oil over the rabbit and sprinkle generously with salt and pepper. Add the potatoes and mix well. Toss the rabbit joints or use a wooden spoon to cover the joints in the mixture.

3 Bake in the oven for 35 minutes. Pour the wine into the dish. Baste the rabbit in wine and pan juices. Bake 15 to 25 minutes more, uncovered, or until the meat is cooked through and the juices have noticeably reduced. Adjust the cooking time according to the size of the rabbit. Transfer to a serving plate, remove and discard the garlic and rosemary. Serve immediately.

Rabbit Fricassee

Coniglio in Fricassea

My mother never used cream to thicken sauces—it was too valuable! Instead, she often used eggs and lemon juice. That same method is used in this delicious recipe. Serve this with potatoes or toasted bread.

PREPARATION TIME: 30 minutes / **COOKING TIME:** 40 minutes / **SERVES:** 4

¼ cup plus 2 tablespoons olive oil ◆ 4½-pound rabbit, skinned and cleaned
All-purpose flour, for coating ◆ 1 cup cooked Soffritto (see page 54), still in pan
2 sprigs fresh rosemary ◆ 4 large garlic cloves, peeled and lightly crushed by hand
½ cup dry white wine ◆ Yolk of 1 large egg ◆ Juice of 1 medium lemon
Salt to taste ◆ Freshly ground black pepper to taste

◆

1 Heat the olive oil in a large skillet over medium heat.

2 While the oil is heating, cut the rabbit into large pieces and lightly coat in flour.

3 Place the rabbit in oil and fry, turning occasionally, until golden brown on all sides (about 5 minutes).

4 Add the Soffritto to the skillet with the rosemary and garlic and heat over medium heat, stirring frequently, for a few minutes.

5 Stir in the wine, reduce the heat to low, and cook for another 20 minutes or until the rabbit is cooked through and the meat comes away from the bone easily. Remove from the heat.

6 Transfer the rabbit to a work surface. Remove and discard the bones. Cut the meat into bite-size pieces.

7 Stirring constantly, add the egg yolk and lemon juice to the Soffritto. Add salt and pepper to taste.

8 Put the rabbit pieces back into the skillet, coat with the Soffritto mixture. Serve immediately.

chapter five
Dolci
DESSERTS

Roasted Strawberries with Balsamic Vinegar
Fragole al Balsamico

This is an extremely simple but delicious dessert that takes little time to prepare. The sweetness of the strawberries contrasts beautifully with the sharpness of the balsamic vinegar.

PREPARATION TIME: 10 minutes / **COOKING TIME:** 15 minutes / **SERVES:** 4

6 cups fresh strawberries ◆ ¼ cup balsamic vinegar
1 tablespoon superfine sugar

◆

1 Preheat the oven to 400°F.

2 Trim and wash the strawberries. Place on a baking tray. Drizzle with the vinegar. Sprinkle the sugar over the strawberries.

3 Bake for 15 minutes. Serve warm or chilled.

Mama says:
These strawberries taste delicious when served with fresh vanilla ice cream or a little whipped cream.

Jelly Tart
Crostata di Marmellata

The secret to this recipe is to use the best (preferably homemade) jam you can find.
Our favorite jams are made from fresh apricots or plums.

PREPARATION TIME: 35 minutes / **COOKING TIME:** 20 to 25 minutes / **SERVES:** 6

3 cups all-purpose flour ◆ 1 heaped teaspoon baking powder ◆ 2 large eggs
¾ cup sugar ◆ ½ cup (1 stick) butter ◆ Pinch of salt
Finely grated peel of ½ organic lemon and ½ organic orange
1 cup Homemade Jelly (see page 149) or other strong-flavored, good-quality jelly
About 2 tablespoons milk or 1 egg white, to glaze

◆

1 Preheat the oven to 350°F.

2 Grease a 10-inch round tart pan. Set aside.

3 Put the flour, baking powder, eggs, sugar, butter, salt, and lemon and orange peels together in a bowl and mix thoroughly to a firm dough. Take out of the bowl and roll out flat to a thickness of ¼ inch. Cut and line the greased tart pan. Press the dough into the pan.

4 Spread the jam over the pastry. The jam should be at least ¾ inch deep. Add more, if desired.

5 Roll out and cut the remains of the pastry into ¼-inch strips. Lay across the tart in a lattice pattern. Brush with a little egg white or milk to glaze.

6 Bake for 20 to 30 minutes or until the pastry is light golden in color and has started to pull away from the edge of the pan.

7 Remove from the oven and let cool completely before serving.

Fried Cinnamon Rice Balls
Fritelle di San Giuseppe

San Giuseppe is Father's Day in Italy, and it falls on March 19. In Tuscany, these rice balls are made to celebrate the day. This is a delicious dish any time of the year, and it's a good way to use any rice pudding you have left over.

PREPARATION TIME: 5 minutes / **COOKING TIME:** 5 minutes / **MAKES:** 12 balls

About 1 to 2 cups sunflower or vegetable oil, for frying ◆ 1½ cups Cinnamon and Orange Rice Pudding (see page 136) ◆ 2 large eggs, separated ◆ ¼ cup vin Santo About 1 tablespoon superfine sugar, to dust ◆ Ground cinnamon, to dust

◆

1 Fill a large, deep saucepan with 4 to 6 inches of oil. Heat over medium heat until very hot.

2 If necessary, thicken the rice pudding by placing it in a saucepan and heating it over low heat, stirring constantly until thick.

3 In a small bowl, lightly beat the egg yolks. Place them in the rice pudding. Add the vin Santo and stir to mix.

4 In a medium bowl, whisk the egg whites until stiff. Gently fold into the rice pudding with a spoon.

5 Drop large tablespoons of the rice pudding mixture into the hot oil. Do not overcrowd the pan. Fry, turning frequently, until the balls are golden brown on all sides (about 2 to 3 minutes). Transfer the fried balls to paper towels to blot any excess oil. Repeat until all the rice pudding is fried.

6 Dust the balls with sugar and a little cinnamon and serve immediately.

Warm Zabaglione
Zabaglione Caldo

Zabaglione is one of the most traditional Italian desserts around. It was created by a chef in the seventeenth century in Turin, when he accidentally poured fortified sweet wine into egg custard. In some areas of Italy, they eat this dish as a hot breakfast.

PREPARATION TIME: 5 minutes / **COOKING TIME:** 8 minutes / **SERVES:** 4

Yolks of 4 large eggs ◆ **3 tablespoons sugar**
3 tablespoons vin Santo or sweet Marsala wine

◆

1 Fill a saucepan with water and bring to a gentle simmer. Place a heatproof bowl over the pan, letting it rest on the rim of the saucepan. Make sure that the water does not touch the base of the bowl.

2 Place the eggs in the bowl. Whisking constantly, add the sugar and vin Santo or sweet Marsala wine.

3 Continue to whisk until the mixture has doubled in volume and is smooth, creamy, and pale.

4 Pour into individual serving glasses and chill in the refrigerator for about 3 hours before serving. Store in the refrigerator for up to 2 days.

Cinnamon and Orange Rice Pudding
Budino di Riso

*This was one of my favorite puddings when I was a child. Mama did not always
have the time to stand at the stove, stirring it for the required lengthy period of time.
In an effort to persuade her to make it more frequently, I took over that job as soon
as I was tall enough to do it. Today, we make this at our café. Our patisserie chef,
Stefano Borella, adds a few cardamom pods, chills the rice in a mold, and turns it
out onto a plate. He serves it with stewed seasonal fruits or a fruit coulis.*

PREPARATION TIME: 5 minutes / **COOKING TIME:** 50 minutes / **SERVES:** 4

1 cup arborio rice ◆ ¼ cup superfine sugar
2 cinnamon sticks or 1 heaping teaspoon ground cinnamon
2-inch-long peel of 1 organic orange ◆ ¾ cup heavy cream
2–2½ cups half-and-half ◆ 4 tablespoons honey

◆

1 Place the rice, sugar, cinnamon, orange peel,
cream, and 2 cups half-and-half in a medium,
heavy-bottomed saucepan. Stirring constantly,
bring to a boil over medium heat.

2 Reduce the heat to low and simmer, stirring
constantly, for 20 to 40 minutes or until the rice

is soft. If necessary, add the remaining half-and-
half while it is cooking to prevent the mixture
from drying out.

3 Remove and discard the orange peel. Transfer
the pudding to individual serving bowls, drizzle
with honey, and serve warm.

Chocolate Pudding
Budino Cioccolato

This is a very simple chocolate pudding that is delicious when served with Vanilla Custard Filling (see page 152). Cocoa is used here instead of chocolate for convenience, but make sure that the cocoa used is of a good quality to ensure the best results.

PREPARATION TIME: 5 minutes / **COOKING TIME:** 30 to 40 minutes / **SERVES:** 6 to 8

**2 cups whole milk ◆ 1 cup good-quality cocoa powder
Yolks of 3 large eggs ◆ ½ cup superfine sugar**

◆

1 Preheat the oven to 300°F.

2 Heat the milk in a medium saucepan over medium heat. Whisk in the cocoa powder.

3 In a large bowl, mix together the egg yolks and sugar. Stirring constantly, add the milk mixture, a little at a time.

4 Place a fine sieve over a large bowl. Pour the mixture through the sieve to remove any lumps.

5 Pour the mixture into individual ramekins or one large ovenproof dish.

6 Place the ramekins in a roasting pan and carefully add enough water to the pan so that the water comes three-fourths of the way up the sides of the ramekins. Cover the tops with a sheet of aluminum foil tucked in around the edge. Bake for 30 to 40 minutes, or until the puddings are firm to the touch.

7 Remove from the oven and let cool to room temperature. Place in the refrigerator and chill 3 to 4 hours.

Tiramisu

Tiramisu

*Because this is usually served at a party, this recipe makes a large amount.
Fortunately, it freezes well. It does take time to make, but the results are
well worth the effort.*

PREPARATION TIME: 30 minutes, plus 24 hours to chill / **COOKING TIME:** 0 minutes / **SERVES:** 8 to 10

6 large eggs from free-range hens, separated ◆ 1 cup superfine sugar ◆ 1 cup mascarpone
(available in the specialty cheese section of most grocery stores) ◆ 1 cup heavy cream
1 cup prepared espresso coffee ◆ ⅔ cup Marsala Secco
30 to 40 Savioardi cookies (available at specialty food stores and at some Italian
delicatessens) ◆ Cocoa powder, to dust

◆

1 In a large bowl, blend the egg yolks and sugar together until the mixture is pale and creamy. Stir in the mascarpone.

2 In a small bowl, whip the cream until soft peaks form. Gently stir the whipped cream into the mascarpone mixture.

3 In a medium bowl, whip the egg whites until stiff peaks form. Fold into the mascarpone-cream mixture.

4 Place one third of the mascarpone-cream mixture in an even layer in a glass serving dish, or divide among individual serving glasses.

5 Place the espresso and Marsala in a shallow bowl and stir together. Quickly dip 10 to 13 cookies (enough for a single layer in the dish) into the espresso. Lay the dipped cookies over the mascarpone-cream mixture in the serving dish, or lay two cookies on the cream in each of the serving glasses. (Do not dip more cookies than are required for each layer at one time. The cookies should not be allowed to become soggy as the dish is being prepared.)

6 Repeat in layers until the cookies are finished. Finish the top layer with the remaining cream. Place in the refrigerator and chill for a minimum of six hours and a maximum of 12 hours. Just before serving, dust with cocoa powder.

Baked Cinnamon Cream Puddings
Budino di Crema

This is one of my favorite puddings. Be warned—it's not for the fainthearted or diet-conscious. When I was a child we ate this plain, but it goes beautifully with stewed winter fruits or fresh summer berries. At Caffè Caldesi, our patisserie chef, Stefano Borella, serves it with Roasted Strawberries with Balsamic Vinegar (see page 132).

PREPARATION TIME: 15 minutes / COOKING TIME: 30 to 35 minutes / SERVES: 8 to 10

**Whites of 5 large eggs ◆ 2 cups heavy cream ◆ Finely grated peel of 1 organic orange
1 teaspoon ground cinnamon ◆ ¾ cup superfine sugar**

◆

1 Preheat the oven to 350°F.

2 In a medium bowl, whisk together the egg whites and cream to combine. Let sit 1 minute. Stir in the orange peel, cinnamon, and sugar.

3 Place equal amounts of the mixture in six small ramekins. Place the ramekins in a roasting pan and carefully add enough water to the pan so that the water comes three-fourths of the way up the sides of the ramekins.

4 Bake 30 to 35 minutes or until the puddings are firm to the touch.

5 Remove from the oven and let cool to room temperature. Refrigerate until chilled. (Puddings may be refrigerated up to 2 days.)

Italian Chocolate and Custard Trifle
Zuppa Inglese

This recipe calls for Alchermes, a bright red Italian liqueur made from a secret recipe. Its taste is difficult to define, but it adds a spicy little punch to many Tuscan desserts. If you cannot find Alchermes, use sherry or brandy instead.

PREPARATION TIME: 10 minutes / **COOKING TIME:** 0 minutes / **SERVES:** 8

½ cup water ◆ ½ cup Alchermes liqueur ◆ 30 to 40 Pavesini cookies (available at specialty food stores and Italian delicatessens) ◆ 1 batch Vanilla Custard Filling (see page 152) 1 batch Chocolate Filling (see page 153)

◆

1 In a bowl, mix together the water and Alchermes. Quickly dip 10 to 13 cookies one by one into the liqueur. Lay the cookies in a single layer at the bottom of a large glass trifle dish (use as many cookies as needed). Spread half of the Vanilla Custard Filling in an even layer over the cookies.

2 Dip 10 to 13 more cookies into the liqueur one by on. Place in a single layer over the filling.

3 Place the Chocolate Filling over the cookies in an even layer.

4 Soak the remaining cookies (or as many as needed) in the liqueur. Place in a single layer over the filling.

5 Top with the remaining Vanilla Custard Filling. Refrigerate 6 to 12 hours. Serve chilled.

Mama says:
You could use leftover sponge cake for the cookie layers instead of Pavesini cookies.

Sunday Cake
Torta della Domenico

My mother used to make this on baking days, when the oven outside was really hot. We would go to Mass at 11:00 a.m. and come back to enjoy a roast, followed by this delicious cake. Mama made it using Alchermes liqueur. The bright red liqueur added zest to both the color and flavor of the cake. If you are unable to locate Alchermes, use the liqueur of your choice instead. This recipe calls for a garnish of confectioners' sugar. On special occasions, however, we used to cover the surface of the cake with additional Vanilla Custard Filling (see page 152), press fresh summer berries into it in concentric circles, and top it with melted apricot jam as a glaze.

PREPARATION TIME: 20 minutes / **COOKING TIME:** 0 minutes / **SERVES:** 6 to 10

**1 Sponge Cake (see page 154) ◆ ½ cup Alchermes liqueur
1 batch Chocolate Filling (see page 153) ◆ 1 batch Vanilla Custard Filling (see page 152)
Cocoa powder and confectioners' sugar to dust**

◆

1 Cut the Sponge Cake into three disks of equal size and thickness.

2 Place the liqueur in a shallow bowl. Soak one disk in liqueur, then place it on a serving platter and spread the Chocolate Filling on top.

3 Place another disk, soaked in the liqueur, on top of the Chocolate Filling. Cover with the Vanilla Custard Filling. Place the third disk on top of the Vanilla Custard Filling. Sprinkle with cocoa powder and confectioners' sugar.

Mama says:
For a decorative effect, lay a doily over the sponge Cake, cover it with confectioners' sugar, and carefully peel off the doily.

Raspberry and Amaretto Roulade
Salami di Lampone Amaretto

We ate this on Sundays or to celebrate special occasions. I helped my mother to roll the roulade up—it frequently cracked but still looked great covered with icing sugar. My mother used to use Alcharmes, a bright red colored liqueur. Nowadays we use Amaretto or rum instead.

PREPARATION TIME: 30 minutes / **COOKING TIME:** 10 minutes / **SERVES:** 4 to 6

About ½ tablespoon butter ◆ 1 cup all-purpose flour
4 large eggs, separated ◆ ¾ cup sugar ◆ About 2 tablespoons Alchermes or Amaretto
7 ounces raspberries ◆ About 4 tablespoons confectioner's sugar to decorate

◆

1 Preheat the oven to 300°F.

2 Line a 10 x 16-inch baking tray with baking paper. Lightly grease the baking paper with butter. Sprinkle about 2 tablespoons flour onto the paper. Shake to distribute and then shake off any excess flour. Set aside.

3 In a medium bowl, beat together the egg yolks and sugar until light and fluffy.

4 In a small bowl, whisk the egg whites until stiff. Gently fold into the egg yolk mixture.

5 Sift the flour. Gently fold into the egg mixture, then pour the mixture into the baking tray. Gently spread into an even layer.

6 Bake 8 to 10 minutes or until golden brown. Remove from the oven. Transfer the paper and cake to a wire rack. Cover with a kitchen towel and let cool.

7 Drizzle the Alchermes or Amaretto onto the cake. Scatter over the raspberries.

8 Beginning at one narrow end, carefully roll up the cake, unpeeling the baking paper as you roll. The finished cake should resemble a Jelly Roll.

9 Transfer to a serving dish and sprinkle with confectioners' sugar and serve.

Pinenut and Raison Cake
Torta di Pinoli e Livetta

In Italy it is common to use sachets of pre-mixed baking powder and vanilla flavoring for all baking. Since they also contain preservatives and are not readily available outside Italy, we use baking powder and vanilla bean seeds or extract instead. This cake is very easy to make and can have fruit, such as plums, pears, or even strawberries, added to it. Simply push the freshly cut fruit into the batter in the baking pan before cooking

PREPARATION TIME: 15 minutes / **COOKING TIME:** 25 to 30 minutes / **SERVES:** 6

7 tablespoons butter, divided ◆ ¾ cup superfine sugar ◆ 3 eggs, lightly beaten
⅔ cup milk ◆ 2 cups all-purpose flour ◆ ½ teaspoon grated peel of organic lemon
1 sachet *lievito* (available at specialty food stores and some Italian delicatessens)
or 2 heaped teaspoons baking powder and vanilla seeds from 1 bean
2 tablespoons pine nuts ◆ 2 tablespoons raisins

◆

1 Preheat the oven to 350°F. Grease an 8-inch round springform pan with 1 tablespoon butter.

2 In a large bowl, cream the remaining butter and sugar. Blend in the eggs and milk. Stir in the flour, lemon peel, and *lievito*. Mix well.

3 Place a thin layer of batter in the pan. Sprinkle evenly with the pine nuts and raisins, then top with the remaining batter.

4 Bake 25 to 30 minutes or until a cocktail stick inserted into the cake's center comes out clean. Let the cake cool in the pan before serving.

Fried Little Pastries

Cenci

Cenci, sometimes called chiacchiere *or* bugia *in different parts of Italy, are made at Carnevale time. They are eaten on our Pancake day when you are supposed to be eating the last of the fattier foods for Lent. Vin Santo is a dessert wine that my father, and most Italians, made at home from semi-dried grapes.*

PREPARATION TIME: 40 minutes / **COOKING TIME:** 2 minutes
MAKES: about 30 to 40 pastries

2½ cups all-purpose flour ◆ 2 medium eggs, beaten ◆ ⅓ cup superfine sugar
1 tablespoon vin Santo ◆ ½ sachet lievito or 2 level teaspoons of baking powder
Grated peel of 1 small organic orange ◆ ⅔ stick butter
About 2 to 3 cups sunflower or vegetable oil ◆ 2 tablespoons confectioners' sugar
2 heaping teaspoons cinnamon

◆

1 Place the flour, eggs, sugar, vin Santo, lievito, and orange peel in a large bowl. Rub in the butter and using your hands, blend the mixture to make a dough.

2 Place enough oil in a large saucepan to form a 3-inch layer. Heat over medium heat.

3 While the oil is heating, transfer the dough to a pastry board or other work surface. Cut the dough into four pieces and then using a rolling pin, roll the quarters of dough into a ¼-inch-thick sheet.

4 Cut the dough into 2 x 1-inch strips. Put the strips in hot oil (do not crowd the pan). Fry until golden brown on both sides (about 2 minutes). Transfer the fried strips to paper towels to blot any excess oil. Repeat until all the strips are fried.

5 Place the confectioners' sugar in a shallow bowl. Toss the fried strips in the confectioners' sugar. Place on a serving plate and sprinkle with cinnamon. Serve.

Ciambellone

Ciambellone

Every Easter, Mama made Ciambellone, a traditional holiday cake. It is in the shape of a ring, and traditionally it's eaten with vin Santo or dipped in caffè latte for breakfast. My cousin Gina makes this using whipped egg whites, which results in a cake lighter than my mother's. Here, we're giving Gina's recipe. It calls for Pane di Angeli, a cook's sachet of baking powder and vanilla extract that is available at most Italian bakeries and delicatessens. The sachet really helps to make a good Italian cake. If it is not available, substitute one teaspoon baking powder and 2 to 3 drops of vanilla extract. Potato flour is also called for here. It is available in most specialty food stores and in some grocery stores. If you cannot locate it, use cornstarch instead.

PREPARATION TIME: 15 minutes / **COOKING TIME:** 35 minutes / **SERVES:** 10

1 cup (2 sticks) butter ◆ Scant 1½ cups superfine sugar ◆ 4 large eggs
2 cups all-purpose flour ◆ Generous ⅓ cup potato flour or cornstarch
Grated peel of 1 medium organic lemon ◆ 4–6 tablespoons milk
1 sachet *Pane di Angeli* or 2 teaspoon baking powder plus 2 to 3 drops vanilla extract

◆

1 Preheat the oven to 350°F.

2 Lightly grease a baking ring mold. Set aside.

3 In a large bowl, cream together the butter and sugar until the mixture is creamy and pale in color.

4 Stir in the egg yolks, all-purpose flour, potato flour or cornstarch, lemon peel, and 4 tablespoons milk. If the mixture is too thick, stir in 1 to 2 more tablespoons milk. Stir in the *Pane di Angeli* or baking powder and vanilla extract, if using.

5 In a medium bowl, whisk the egg whites until peaks form. Fold the egg whites into the batter.

6 Pour the batter into the mold. Bake for 20 minutes or until golden brown and springy to the touch.

Almond Cookies
Cantuccini

To dunk or not to dunk—that is the question! When we visit family, we are usually greeted with a glass of vin Santo, a dessert wine, and cantuccini (small cookies) or cantucci (large cookies). Some people prefer not to dunk their cookies in the wine because they feel that the little crumbs left at the bottom of the glass ruin the beverage. We, however, love to dunk our cantuccini in vin Santo—the cookies soak up the liqueur beautifully, resulting in a wonderful flavor and a soft texture. What is the correct way to enjoy these treats? As we say in Italy, "Come vuoi"—"It's up to you."

PREPARATION TIME: 20 minutes / **COOKING TIME:** 25 minutes / **SERVES:** 6 to 8

¾ cup whole blanched almonds, toasted ◆ 1⅔ cups all-purpose flour
¾ cup superfine sugar ◆ 1 teaspoon baking powder ◆ 2 large eggs, lightly beaten
1 teaspoon vanilla extract ◆ 1 teaspoon grated peel of an organic lemon
Confectioners' sugar to dust

◆

1 Preheat the oven to 350°F. Lightly toast the almonds, being careful not to burn them.

2 In a large bowl, mix together the flour, sugar, and baking powder. Stir in the almonds.

3 Add the eggs, vanilla extract, and lemon peel. Stir to form a smooth, thick dough.

4 Divide the mixture into thirds. Make each third into a sausage shape by rolling it in confectioners' sugar, using your hands.

5 Place the rolls on a cookie sheet and flatten slightly, using your hands. Bake for 20 minutes or until golden brown.

6 Remove from the oven. Cut each roll diagonally into ½-inch-wide strips. Spread the strips in a single layer on a cookie sheet and return to the oven. Bake for another 2 to 3 minutes. Use two trays if necessary. Let cool before serving.

Homemade Jelly
Marmellata

When the fruit was ripe on the trees, we picked as much as we could before the birds got to it. We had excesses of damsons, plums, and peaches, and inevitably, after we'd eaten our fill of them, Mama would turn the remaining fruit into jelly. We used the jelly throughout the year to spread onto bread, cakes, and other delicacies. When it was cooking, the jelly splattered everywhere. I remember being covered with tiny jelly burns. We loved the finished product, though, and I always considered my "battle scars" a small price to pay for it. Tuscan jelly is quite runny—we didn't really worry about it setting, so we just boiled it and preserved it.

PREPARATION TIME: 15 minutes / **COOKING TIME:** 90 minutes / **MAKES:** 5 cups

2¼ pounds very ripe plums, damsons, or peaches ◆ 13 cups superfine sugar

◆

1 Remove and discard the pits from the fruit. Place the fruit in a large, heavy-bottomed saucepan. Add the sugar. Bring to a boil over medium heat. Boil 40 to 50 minutes.

2 Turn off the heat and let the jam cool until it is warm.

3 Place the jelly in sterile jars of any size and cover each with circles of waxed paper. Seal tightly with lids.

4 As a precaution against the jam becoming moldy, half-fill a large roasting pan with cold water. Place the sealed jars in the pan and put in the oven at a low temperature for 15 minutes. This will make a vacuum between the lid and the jelly.

5 Remove the jars from the pan and set aside to cool. Store in a cool, dark place. The jelly may be kept for up to 3 months.

Pine Nut–Caramel Crunch
Croccante con Pinoli

My mother used to make this as a treat whenever we had an abundance of pine nuts. As children, we were allowed to help "smash it up" and eat it, of course. It's a tooth cracker, so watch out.

PREPARATION TIME: 2 minutes / **COOKING TIME:** 10 minutes / **SERVES:** 4 to 6

About 1 tablespoon vegetable oil ◆ 2 cups superfine sugar
¼ cup water ◆ 2 cups pine nuts

◆

1 Grease a marble or granite slab or a nonstick baking tray with vegetable oil. Set aside.

2 Put the sugar and water in a medium saucepan. Bring to a boil over medium heat. Reduce the heat to medium-low and simmer for about 10 to 15 minutes, until the mixture caramelizes (turns thick and golden brown). Avoid stirring the mixture while you wait for the color to change.

3 Add the pine nuts. Cook, stirring constantly, for 1 minute. Make sure you don't let the pine nuts burn.

4 Pour onto the slab or baking tray and let cool to room temperature.

5 Using a small hammer covered in a clean cloth, smash the mixture into small pieces.

Sweet Bread with Raisins
Ciaccia Dolce

My father used to hang bunches of sweet grapes to dry on wires between the rafters in the house. We had our own vineyards, so we sold a lot of grapes, but always kept some for ourselves to make vin Santo or to enjoy as snacks. Although my father never drank, we kept the vin Santo mainly to offer to guests.

PREPARATION TIME: 45 to 75 minutes / **COOKING TIME:** 20 to 25 minutes / **SERVES:** 4

**2¼ cups warm water ◆ 1 ounce fresh yeast or ¾-ounce package dry yeast
4¼ cups self-rising flour, sifted ◆ Pinch of salt ◆ 2 tablespoons raisins,
soaked in orange juice or water for ½ hour and drained ◆ 1 teaspoon butter
2 tablespoons superfine sugar ◆ 2 tablespoons extra virgin olive oil**

◆

1 Place the water in a large bowl. Stir in the yeast.

2 In a large bowl, mix together the flour and salt. Make a well in the center of the flour. Pour in the yeast-water mixture. Using a round-bladed knife mix until all the flour is incorporated, adding more water, if required.

3 Transfer the mixture to a pastry board or other work surface. Using your hands, knead until the dough is soft but firm (add more water if necessary). Add the raisins and mix well.

4 Return dough to the bowl. Cover with a damp kitchen towel and let sit in a warm, draft-free place until the dough has doubled in size (about 30 minutes to 1 hour).

5 Preheat the oven to 400°F.

6 Grease a baking tray with butter.

7 Transfer the dough to a pastry board or other work surface. Using a rolling pin, flatten the dough into 1 large loaf or 2 small ¾-inch-thick oval loaves.

8 Place the loaf on the baking tray, then with your finger tips make little dents all over the bread to create pockets for oil and sugar. Drizzle over the oil, then sprinkle with the sugar.

9 Bake for 20 to 25 minutes or until the bread is golden brown.

Vanilla Custard Filling
Crema Pasticierra

Mama would make this for special occasions. It was often used as an ingredient for other dishes such as Italian Chocolate and Custard Trifle (see page 141) and Sunday Cake (see page 143).

PREPARATION TIME: 10 minutes / **COOKING TIME:** 15 minutes / **MAKES:** 3 cups

Yolks of 5 large eggs from free-range (preferably corn-fed) hens
¼ cup cornstarch ◆ ½ cup superfine sugar ◆ 3 cups whole milk
1 vanilla pod ◆ 2-inch-long peel of 1 organic lemon

1 In a medium-sized bowl, cream together the egg yolks, cornstarch, and sugar until the mixture is smooth and pale. Set aside.

2 Place the milk, vanilla pod, and lemon peel in a large saucepan. Bring to a boil over medium heat. Remove from the heat. Remove the vanilla pod and lemon peel and set aside.

3 Stirring constantly, slowly add the milk mixture to the egg yolk mixture. If you'd like a strong vanilla flavor, place the vanilla pod in the mixture until the desired flavor is reached.

4 Transfer the mixture to the saucepan in which the milk was cooked. Stirring constantly, bring to a boil over medium-low heat. Cook, stirring constantly, until the mixture thickens (about 5 to 7 minutes).

5 Pour the mixture into a clean bowl. Seal the bowl with plastic wrap to prevent the mixture from developing a skin.

6 Set aside to cool to room temperature. Store in the refrigerator until needed. It will keep for up to 2 days.

Chocolate Filling
Cioccolato al Cacao

Once each month we had cocoa powder and my mama would make Budino di Cioccolato or this chocolate filling. It was used in the Sunday Cake (see page 143) or Italian Chocolate and Custard Trifle (see page 141), and Roberto and I loved it. Chocolate was a rarity and we savored every bite!

PREPARATION TIME: 5 minutes / **COOKING TIME:** 15 minutes / **MAKES:** 3 to 4 cups

¾ **cup superfine sugar** ◆ **2 cups cocoa powder containing 70 percent cocoa solids**
3 tablespoons cornstarch ◆ **3 cups whole milk**

◆

1 In a large bowl, mix together the sugar, cocoa, and cornstarch. Add 1 cup milk and stir to blend.

2 Place the remaining milk in a medium saucepan. Bring to a boil over medium heat. Immediately remove from the heat. Stirring constantly, slowly pour the milk into the cocoa mixture, a little at a time.

3 Transfer the mixture to the saucepan in which the milk was heated. Stirring constantly, bring to a gentle boil over medium-low heat. Cook, stirring constantly, for 3 to 5 minutes or until the mixture has thickened.

4 Pour the mixture into a clean bowl. Seal the surface of the chocolate filling with baking paper to prevent the mixture from developing a skin. Set aside to cool to room temperature. Refrigerate until needed. Store in the refrigerator for up to 3 days.

Sponge Cake
Pan d'Espagna

This was the basic sponge cake recipe that Mama used in a variety of desserts, including Italian Chocolate and Custard Trifle (see page 141) and Sunday Cake (see page 143).

PREPARATION TIME: 15 minutes / **COOKING TIME:** 35 minutes / **SERVES:** 6

1 teaspoon butter ◆ 5 large eggs, separated
⅔ cup superfine sugar ◆ 1¼ cups all-purpose flour, sifted ◆ 1 tablespoon baking powder
2 teaspoons grated peel of organic orange or lemon (if desired)

◆

1 Preheat the oven to 350°F.

2 Grease an 8-inch round springform pan with the butter. Set aside.

3 In a medium-sized bowl, cream together the egg yolks and sugar until light and fluffy.

4 In another medium-sized bowl, whisk the egg whites until stiff. Fold the whites into the egg yolk and sugar mixture.

5 Sift the flour and baking powder together, then very gently fold into the egg mixture with a wooden spoon. Also fold in the grated peel, if using. Pour the batter into the pan.

6 Bake for 30 to 35 minutes or until a toothpick inserted in the center of the cake comes out clean.

7 Remove the cake from the pan, place on a wire rack, and allow to cool.

Soft Sienese Cookies
Ricciarelli

This recipe calls for a mixture of sweet and bitter almonds, which are available in Italy. If you are unable to locate either of these, you can use plain almonds instead.

PREPARATION TIME: 15 minutes / **COOKING TIME:** 10 to 15 minutes / **MAKES:** about 15 cookies

---

4 tablespoons all-purpose flour, sifted
2½ cups ground sweet almonds ◆ ⅔ cup ground bitter almonds
1½ cups confectioners' sugar ◆ 1 teaspoon baking powder
Whites of 6 large eggs ◆ ⅓ cup superfine sugar

◆

1 Preheat the oven to 300°F.

2 Cover a cookie sheet with baking paper. Set aside.

3 In a large mixing bowl, mix together the flour, almonds, half of the confectioners' sugar, and baking powder.

4 In a medium-sized bowl, whisk the egg whites until stiff, adding the superfine sugar as you go. Fold into the almond-sugar mixture.

5 Take two spoons and form quenelles (raised oval shapes) by pushing the mixture between the two spoons and then dropping them gently into a bowl of the remaining confectioners' sugar to coat them. Remove each quenelle and place on the cookie sheet, spaced apart.

6 Bake for 10 to 15 minutes or until golden brown. Remove from the oven and let cool on a wire rack before serving. They can be stored for up to a week in an airtight container.

Glossary

Aioli: A dressing or dipping sauce made from oil, egg yolks, seasonings, and garlic cloves.

Albacore: A species of tuna fish found in the West Indies.

Alchermes: A red Italian liqueur used in desserts. Sherry or brandy may be used as a substitute.

Alla brace: Charcoal-grilled.

All'aglione: Heavily flavored with garlic.

Alle briciole: Served with bread crumbs.

Antipasti: Starters or appetizers (hors d'oeuvres) served cold or hot.

Arborio rice: A round-grained rice capable of absorbing fluid while cooking without losing texture. It is the preferred type of rice for risottos.

Baccalà: Dried salt cod.

Balsamic vinegar: Wine vinegar sweetened and mellowed by being aged in wooden casks.

Béchamel sauce: A plain white sauce given extra flavor by infusing the milk with vegetables and seasonings.

Bruschetta: Slices of bread toasted with garlic and olive oil.

Cannellini beans: White haricot beans, usually available canned or dried, used in soups and stews.

Canneloni: Large pasta tubes usually stuffed with savory fillings and baked.

Cantucci: Almond cookies served with sweet wine.

Carnevale: Carnival celebrations in the week preceding Lent, culminating in Shrove Tuesday (Mardi Gras).

Cenci: Fried sweet pastries.

Chiodini: Tiny wild mushrooms used in cooking in Italy.

Ciambellone: A ring-shaped cake flavored with lemon peel and traditionally served at Easter.

Contorni: Side dishes.

Crostini: Small pieces of toast with toppings served as antipasti.

Ditalini rigate: Short, ridged pasta used in soups.

Dolcelatte: Creamy-textured, off-white cheese with blue-green veins running through it.

Dolci: Sweets and desserts.

Fagiolini: Green (French) beans.

Farfalle: Butterfly or bow-shaped pasta.

Fava beans: Broad beans.

Fettunta: Garlic bread.

Fiammiferi: Tiny wild mushrooms used in cooking in Italy.

Fricassée: White stew of chicken, rabbit, or veal in which the meat is first fried, then cooked in stock and finished with cream and egg yolks.

Fritelle: Pancake.

Fritelle di budino di riso: Balls of sweet rice pudding stiffened with beaten eggs, dropped into a skillet, and cooked like pancakes.

Frittata: Omelette.

Gallina con uva e pinoli: Chicken with grapes and pine nuts.

Gnocchi: Small dumplings made with mashed potatoes or semolina flour.

Lasagna: Flat sheets of egg pasta. Lasagne verdi is made with spinach.

Lievito: Yeast generated from flour, water, and hops or grape skins.

Marsala: A sweet, fortified wine. Marsala Secco is a drier variety.

Mascarpone: A rich cream cheese used most frequently in making desserts.

Mozzarella: A soft cheese originally made from buffalo milk, with a notable melting quality. Cheaper versions of the cheese are made from cow milk.

Nobile di Montepulciano: One of Italy's highest-quality red wines.

Offal: Edible internal organs and body parts of cattle and poultry. In Italy, offal is called "la cucina povera" (cuisine of the poor) because of its relatively low cost.

Olive oil, extra-virgin: The oil produced from the first cold pressing of the olives.

Panzanella: A Tuscan salad made with cucumber, tomato, and moistened bread.

Pappardelle: Large, flat pasta noodles.

Parmesan (Parmigiano): Hard, strong-flavored cheese usually grated or shaved onto dishes as a seasoning. True Parmigiano Reggiano is manufactured from milk coming from specific regions of northern Italy, under stringent conditions. Cheaper versions are available grated.

Passito: Sweet wine made from raisins.

Pastaiola: A person who makes and sells fresh pasta.

Pecorino: A cheese made from sheep milk. It is sold fresh, medium, or mature. The fresh cheese does not keep well, but the mature version is used much like Parmesan.

Penne: Quill-shaped pasta cut diagonally to catch more sauce.

Pesto: A dressing made from pine nuts, basil, olive oil, and cheese.

Pici: A thick spaghetti characteristic of Tuscan cuisine.

Polenta: A coarsely ground corn (maize) meal cooked similar to oatmeal.

Porcini: Edible mushrooms that can be gathered in the wild or bought dried.

Primi: First courses.

Prosciutto: Parma ham. A raw smoked ham served finely sliced.

Prosecco: A sparkling wine drunk as an apéritif.

Radicchio: A red leafed member of the chicory family, with a slightly bitter taste.

Ragù: A sauce of ground meat and tomatoes, usually served with pasta.

Ricciarelli: Soft Sienese cookies made with almonds.

Ricotta: A soft, fresh cheese made from whey after its separation from the curd.

Rigatoni: Short, hollow pasta tubes.

Savioardi cookies: Sponge fingers used in assembling tiramisu and other desserts.

Secondi: Main courses.

Soffrito: Carrots, celery, onions, garlic, and herbs fried in olive oil and used as a base for sauces, soups, and casseroles.

Spaghetti: Pasta made in solid strings.

Tagliatelle: Long ribbons of egg pasta.

Tegame: Terra-cotta cooking pot with lid.

Tiramisu: Literally "pick-me-up," a rich dessert of coffee-flavored cream, eggs, Mascarpone cheese, and Savioardi cookies.

Tomatoes, sun-blushed: Half-dried tomatoes.

Torta al Domenico: A sponge cake traditionally baked on Sundays and served as a dessert.

Vendemmia: The grape harvest.

Vin Santo: A sweet wine made with half-dried grapes.

Zabaglione: Dessert consisting of egg yolks and sugar, flavored with Marsala or other fortified wines and cooked over a double boiler.

00 flour: Fine ground wheat flour used in bread and pasta making.

Zuppa Inglese: Literally "English soup," the Italian version of trifle.

Index

Picture Credits

Mama says...
Tuscan villagers eat with the seasons. Use only the very freshest ingredients to get the best results from your recipes.